# CHASING A DREAM

## Journeys into the heartland of Tribal India

First published in India in 2014 by CinnamonTeal Publishing

Copyright © 2014 Prosenjit Das Gupta

ISBN 978–93–83175–91–8

Typesetting and Cover design: CinnamonTeal Publishing

Photographs: Prosenjit Das Gupta

CinnamonTeal Publishing
Plot No 16, Housing Board Colony
Gogol, Margao
Goa 403601 India
www.cinnamonteal.in

# CHASING A DREAM

## Journeys into the heartland of Tribal India

## Prosenjit Das Gupta

CINNAMONTEAL PUBLISHING

*Dedicated to some of the finest and kindest people in India*

To the late Sriman Baghel and Jaidev Baghel, Masoo Netam, Belgur Mandavi, the Sirdar of Jharavahi, Kutano Gamang, Balaram Ranahathi and many others.

# Contents

Acknowledgements     9

Preface     13

Introduction     17

The First Foray     26

Through Elwin's Eyes     38

Chasing a Dream: Abujhmarh     50

In Elwin's foot-steps     67

Chhota Dongar     71

Days and nights in Bastar     79

Of Bhaku and Ghotuls     90

Into the Heart of Abujhmarh     100

The Ganjam Interlude     117

One Last Time     131

Elwin: At Home and at Work     136

Elwin: In the Field     152

Finally, the Baiga     160

Epilogue     163

Bibliography     166

# Acknowledgements

The pool of information and experiences that has largely led to this book would not have been possible without the personal affection and unstinted support – often at personal inconvenience – that Jaidev Baghel of Kondagaon extended to me from 1973, when I first met him, till 1994, when we had our last outing together amidst the forests, streams and hills of Bastar. The warm welcome and ready hospitality that I had received from his father, the late Shriman, and his mother, and indeed from all the members of his family – Sonaru (his elder brother), Godhni (his sister), his other elder sisters, his paternal aunt (whom I knew only as 'Bubu') was humbling.

The other pillar on which this book stands is Ashok, the youngest son of Dr. Verrier Elwin. I first met Ashok in October 1977, on a visit – rather, a pilgrimage, so to speak – to their Shillong residence in the Khasi Hills of northeast India. It is here that Dr. Elwin's collection of books, handicrafts and photographs are kept. I went back again in 2000, 2002 and 2004 when I had several days of discussions with Ashok, who has been most understanding and supportive. He seemed to intuitively understand my hunger for information and readily gave me access to several books and tour notes by Dr. Elwin, as well as a lot of photographs, many of which are still unpublished. On my second visit, I was allowed to browse at will through the personal diaries of Dr. Elwin, which helped corroborate certain aspects of Dr. Elwin's life and work that I had merely guessed and threw up several new features. Ashok's remembrances of the times shared with his father in Shillong have been very valuable. He also led me to several people connected with Dr. Elwin, such as Someshwar Lahiri who had been Dr. Elwin's personal secretary between 1955 and 1964, in Shillong. I am much beholden to Mrs. Lila Elwin, widow of Dr. Elwin, (now unfortunately no more) for sharing some of her recollections of Dr. Elwin's 'ashram' at Patangarh and his later tours in Arunachal Pradesh (then known as the North East Frontier Agency). The hospitality of Ashok and his wife has been most warm and enjoyable.

For the basic facts and information on his career in India, I have relied on Elwin's autobiography, *The Tribal World of Verrier Elwin* (later mentioned as *TWVE*), supplemented to some extent by Ramachandra Guha's *Savaging the Civilised* (Oxford University Press, 1999). Unfortunately, when I finally got down to researching additional biographical materials on Dr. Elwin for this book, many people who had known Dr. Verrier Elwin at first hand, such as Prof. N.K. Bose, Dr. Sachin Roy, Dr. Bivas Das Sashtri, or had worked with him in the field, such as Prof. Ashutosh Bhattacharya or Sunderlal Narmada Prasad, had passed away. So had his compatriots and supporters such as W.V. Grigson, W.G. Archer, A.N. Mitchell, Dr. J.H. Hutton and Christoff von Fürer Haimendorf. Nonetheless, it was possible to get some glimpses of Dr. Elwin's remarkable personality from Mr. Someshwar Lahiri (who overcame his initial reluctance to discuss with a total stranger about his very personal and still very acute feelings for Dr. Elwin) and from Mr. Sushanta Chattopadhyay, cinematographer par excellence with the Anthropological Survey of India (now retired), who had worked for a short spell in 1946 with Dr. Elwin in the Singhbhum district of Bihar (now under Jharkhand). I am deeply grateful to them. I have also much benefitted from the recollections of and discussions with Khwaja Abdur Razzaq, Superintending Anthropologist with the Anthropological Survey of India (now retired) concerning Dr. Elwin and specifically about Razzaq's own field researches on the Saora tribe of Ganjam (on whom Dr. Elwin had written the seminal *The Religion of an Indian Tribe*).

I am deeply indebted to Ms. Sheleen Folkes of the Oriental and India Office Collections in London and Mr. Hedley Sutton of the OIOC Reference Services at the British Library, London, for guiding me through the archival materials about Dr. Elwin available with the respective organisations. They truly realised the predicament of a researcher far away in India who could not personally access these materials. I am much obliged to Kabir Singh for following up, in spite of personal inconvenience, on some of these materials at the British Library. I would like to place on record my sincere thanks to Dr. Walworth of Merton College, Oxford (where Elwin had studied in the 1920's) for dealing with my queries, and to Mr. Julian Reid, Archivist at Merton, for furnishing certain important details about Elwin that I had asked for. I am also obliged to Mr. Martin Wooller of the Indian Civil Service Association, U.K., for filling in information about Grigson, Archer and Mitchell that were most useful. I must acknowledge with thanks the assistance of Ms. Yaye Tang of the Library of the School of Oriental and African Studies, London, for furnishing copies of some notes by Dr. Christoff von Fürer Haimendorf, who carried out anthropological studies almost contemporaneously with Dr. Elwin, on the Chenchu and Reddis of the Bison Hills, and was a close acquaintance of his. Many thanks are due to my good friend, Ms. Akane Kitamura, for taking the trouble to obtain from the Tokyo Foreign University a copy of the exhaustive annotated bibliography of Elwin prepared by Prof. Fujii Takeshi, a most valuable document.

In my field visits to the Saora tribal villages in Ganjam (Orissa) between 1977 and 1979, I was greatly assisted by Shri Bhubanananda Bissoyi of Gumma, Shri Giridhari Gomango, then Member of Parliament, who maintained close connections with his roots among the Saora, and by Kutano Gamang who accompanied me to several of the villages near Gumma and on the slopes of Deogiri. I cannot ever forget the assistance I received from Shri Balaram Ranahati of R. Udayagiri, who personally led me to several Saora villages in the hills in that area and was most thoughtful about my welfare.

This book would not have been possible without their ready and warm support.

*Prosenjit Das Gupta*
*Calcutta, 1 March 2014*

# Preface

This story has a dream-like quality even after nearly forty years, when these journeys took place, almost on a whim. It began one summer afternoon in 1965, nearly fifty years ago, in the reading room of a library, and though it started off almost like a day-dream, it quickly had to encounter real people and real situations. The travels were to places and people so far away in time and space, and who have been so long outside the public gaze and attention that one never quite knew when the dream ended and reality intervened. Of course, these regions of India are now better known, and unfortunately for the wrong reasons. It was also ideosyncratic for it concerned a person, Dr. Verrier Elwin, a former clergyman-turned anthropologist, whom I had never seen, although – had I known - I could have met him in Shillong in the early 1960s, and whose footsteps I later followed in Bastar and in the hills and forests of Orissa and central India. But a closer acquaintance with Elwin had to wait for its time till I had roamed those places where live the Muria, Maria and the Saora tribesmen about whom Elwin had written, and met Dr. Elwin's family between 2000 and 2005. The story has a surreal quality, for, at times I feel that what I had seen and experienced in those far-away places in central India was more real and still very much more palpable than my job (till just a few years ago) in my work-place in Calcutta, the daily journeys by bus or taxi, the traffic jams, and the evenings spent in front of the TV.

The centenary of Verrier Elwin came and went almost unnoticed in 2002. In these days of IT and e-commerce, there are not many people, other than those interested in or concerned with anthropology and ethnography, who remember or would like to remember him.

In the nineteenth century and the first four decades of the twentieth century, there were quite a few sections in the British administration who, one way or the other, aided and abetted the oppression and exploitation of the Indian people, and especially the tribal population. Of course, there is no doubt that there was also a significant section that contributed significantly to the well-being of Indians, and to the preservation of their history, language and culture, something that we tend to take so much for granted nowadays. It is a moot point that but for Sir William Jones, James Prinsep, William Carey, David Hare, Lord Curzon, Sir John Marshall, Sir Mortimer Wheeler and many other such persons, we would not have retained the vast trove of manuscripts and artifacts, paintings and temples that India possesses and currently preserves in fairly good condition, and have the education and capacity to enjoy and value them.

The bedrock of this enduring civilisation has been the people, especially the indigenous people, who mingled and mixed with others from within and without the country, on the shores of this vast ocean of humanity, to paraphrase the poet Rabindranath Tagore. While some of our classical texts, in both north and south India, do refer to the indigenous tribes, it was not until E.H. Dalton and later Thurston came out with their reports that the outside world – mentioned here both literally and metaphorically – came to know of them in any detail. H.H. Risley followed with the *Linguistic Survey*, and then came the monographs on the tribes of north-eastern India by J.H. Hutton and J.P. Mills. Our home-grown Sarat Chandra Roy, G.S. Ghurye, Nirmal Kumar Bose and D.N. Majumdar also made notable contributions on some of the tribes in south-central India.

In the middle of all this came Verrier Elwin, the son of a clergyman, a member of the Church of England, and a clergyman himself. He was not the first Englishman to have been deeply influenced by Mahatma Gandhi and to devote himself to the cause of Indians. But his service to the people, especially among the backward tribes of central India, by way of education, health and treatment of leprosy was, if anything, surpassed by his chronicling of the life and cultures of these people. His monographs on the Baiga, the Agaria, the Maria, Muria, and the Saora are not only monumental in size, but also most impressive in range and depth.

The purpose of this book is not to write a biography of Elwin. Elwin had done a good job of that himself, and Ramachandra Guha has recently provided some more documentation. This book narrates a journey – part travelogue, part personal search after a dream and part commentary – of a person who took it into his head to go after Elwin, both literally and metaphorically, and of the sights and sounds, the experiences and impressions that he discovered on his way. It is, therefore, something of a travelogue about places and people that are not commonly written of in India but are very much a part of this great and diverse country. All through, running as an underlying theme, are the studies that Verrier Elwin had done some sixty to seventy years ago on those areas and tribes which impelled me to try and go to the same places to see and experience the same things and events. It was a chase after Elwin in time and space, to confirm to myself the places, the sights and sounds that he had written about, and to see to what extent I could re-construct and understand his life, some sixty years after he had passed away, when the trail had run cold and memories had largely faded. It was an interesting physical and mental challenge.

# 1

# Introduction

The ticket checker at Waltair railway station was a thin scrawny man who laboured through his sheaves of paper and painstakingly wrote out the extension of the rail journey from Waltair to Vizianagram. Twenty-five miles farther on, the train stopped briefly at Vizianagram station, which stood on a sort of embankment at least 50 feet above the level of the town. It was about one-thirty in the afternoon and the sun was beginning to feel a little hot as the tired traveller, looking somewhat out-of-place in that small town in baggy jeans, tousled hair, scruffy whiskered face and a rucksack that had seen happier days over the shoulder, gingerly stepped down from the train onto the platform.

The traveller did not seem to like the first look of Vizianagram with its heat, oppressive even on a winter afternoon. It was a shanty town near the station and a number of scruffy children were rolling over one another in a rough and tumble on the roadside. Yet this would serve as the staging point for the first trip that he would make into what would quite possibly be a completely new world. He eased the rucksack off his shoulder and went into a tea shop for a bit of food and to figure out what would be the best way for him to continue. The *chai-walla* was busy making *puris* to catch the all-important lunch crowd and was as communicative as a clam. All he got out of him was a mutter that a bus to Koraput left every morning and afternoon. The details about the bus's exact timings was, however, left hanging in the air. Eating greasy *puris* and cold vegetable curry normally does not excite people, but the traveller, far from his home, did feel an excitement stirring within as he waited in the awning of the tea-shop for that bus to come. It finally arrived at about three in the afternoon with a rattle in its every conceivable metallic part and jangle in every bit of glass. Much shouting and gesticulation ensued from the waiting crowd of raised and expectant faces as they greeted the bus. The bus conductor managed to impose some semblance of order simply by shoving and pushing and shouting at the top of his voice. Although quite inexperienced in the fine art of boarding a country bus, the very thought of missing the bus – both literally and metaphorically – and having to stay back in Vizianagram, seemed to spur the traveller to scramble up and push his way into a seat next to the driver. Without much ado, the bus got its act together and, managing to hold onto its gear box and crank shaft, soon left the huddle of canister and plywood huts behind. The traveller was now greeted by large stretches of washed green fields, set off by etched black lines of palmyra trees against gently rolling hills that make up the East Godavari and Shrikakulam districts of Andhra.

Thus began my first trip, in the winter of 1970, to Bastar. In truth, however, the journey had originally begun on one ordinary day in the winter of 1965 in the library of Jadavpur University when I was rummaging for some reference books on economics. This book lay half-hidden under a pile of tomes on Indian history, English Literature and the like, seen but discarded for perhaps more interesting topics as college students often do; for it bore little or no relevance to the need for scoring additional marks in the half-yearly tests later that month. What caught my eye was a picture of strange looking wooden masks on the top left and right-hand corners of the cover together with the face of a grey-haired person. It seemed quite unusual and I pulled out the book from under the pile. The dust-cover showed a number of head-dresses and other handicrafts that I had never seen before. In the top centre was the colour-crayon portrait of an elderly man, with longish grey hair and a pair of horn-rimmed spectacles, obviously reading something and solemnly smoking a cigar. The artist had made the smoke curl and swirl around him very convincingly. Below was a figure of the Buddha also swathed in this miasmic cigar smoke. The title read *The Tribal World of Verrier Elwin*.

It was as good a book as any to borrow from the library and upon browsing through I learnt that this elderly person had been born far away in Dover, on the south east coast of England, on 29 August 1902, to an Anglican clergyman and his wife. He was of Scottish and Irish extraction and had been christened with a large mouthful name – Harry Verrier Holman Elwin. He had lost his father when he was only about seven years old, and in spite of a somewhat straitened condition, his mother had tried to bring him up along with his sister and younger brother in the best manner possible. He had received his school education at Dean Close, which had been set up by the father of the well-known poet, James Elroy Fletcher. He had had ample time to browse through the school library and had become particularly attracted to the poetry of Tennyson, Swinburne, Yeats and Wordsworth. He became particularly fond of the latter and visited the Lake District where Wordsworth had long stayed and drawn his inspiration from. Elwin did well enough in school to get admission into Merton College, Oxford, in 1922. There, he studied English Literature and also became involved in prayer meetings and hymn singing and participated in Sunday sermons. He did well enough to become a Charles Oldham Scholar and a Mathew Arnold Prizeman. After getting a First in 1924, he went on take up post-graduate studies in theology. At this time – as the book mentions - he had both formal and informal interactions on religious studies including a brush with the Moral Re-armament movement of which Frank Buchman was a leading light. Although his father had been a staunch Anglican, Elwin was to an extent influenced by the Anglo-Catholicism of some of his friends. He, thus, inculcated in some part the view that the objective of religion was not limited to personal salvation but extended to moral duty towards others and propagating moral virtues. After completing his theological studies, he was formally ordained as an Anglican priest. He spent considerable time in this period of his life fasting and in vigil and prayers. At the same time, as Elwin himself admits in *The Tribal World*, he felt himself drawn to mysticism through the works of William Law and Jacob Boehme. In the process, he also became interested in Hindu mysticism and at about the same time, he was introduced by his friend, Bernard Aluwihare, to the works of Rabindranath Tagore and Gandhi.

*The Tribal World* added that the family on his mother's side had a connection with India. His grandmother had been born in India and one of his maternal uncles had served as a senior military officer. Even amongst his father's relations, there were some that had served in the Indian Civil Service. Thus, Elwin was attracted towards things Indian and particularly to the Indian freedom movement. He found an opportunity to get to India through Father Jack Winslow, who had set up the Christa Seva Sangh near Pune. Elwin decided to join the CSS, which basically had a monastic approach, with emphasis on scholarship rather than proselytising. It was a life of simplicity, even some privation, with time spent in prayers and meditation. In all this, Elwin was motivated by his persistent thoughts of reparations for the exploitation that the British (and perhaps his own family in some way or another) had perpetrated in India. Thus, by November 1927 he had arrived in Pune and started work at the CSS. However, he did not want go out and work as any other missionary did. He was more inclined to study the interaction between Indian and Western mysticism. He came out with a couple of small books, one entitled *Christian Dhyana* (the title makes his interest quite evident) and another on how the teachings of St. Francis of Assisi could be applied in the Indian conditions. As it happened, he met Gandhi in January 1928 and totally fell under his spell. While he was still attached to CSS, he spent considerable time at Sabarmati Ashram in 1930 imbibing both the philosophy and the discipline that Gandhi inculcated in his followers, particularly in relation to cleanliness, chastity, service and a sense of fair play. He increasingly began to feel that there was a dichotomy between the humanity and righteousness that Christianity preached and what the British administration practised in India, particularly with respect to the Indian national movement. His thoughts on these issues were discussed in the book *Christ and Satyagraha*, to highlight how Gandhi's movement was closely akin to the Christian principles of truth and non-violence (who does not remember the New Testament injunction to turn the other cheek!). During this period, he had also come in contact with other senior followers of Gandhi, such as Jamnalal Bajaj and Vallabhbhai Patel, and was advised that if he was to serve India he should work amongst the backward tribes such as Bhils and Gonds. Therefore, he spent some time touring the Bhil areas of western Central Provinces (now Madhya Pradesh) and in other work that Gandhi had assigned him.

While at CSS, he had come in contact with one Shamrao Hivale who, I was to learn later, had been born near Sholapur in Maharashtra, had received his initial education at the Wilson High School in Mumbai, and then at college at Kolhapur, before proceeding to the United Kingdom for initiation into Christian Orders. Shamrao had also been deeply moved by Gandhi's life and teachings and had been advised to get back to India to work among the people. Since Shamrao had no formal education in medicine, he attached himself to an American missionary, Dr. Goheen, at Vengurla, for six months to learn about first aid and treatment of lepers. Shamrao met Elwin in 1931 while visiting Gandhi. Finally, with Shamrao accompanying him, on 28 January 1932, Elwin reached Karanjia, as recommended by the then Bishop of Nagpur; for he was still under the administrative set-up of the Church of England in India. Karanjia is situated about eighteen kilometres west of the pilgrim centre of Amarkantak in Shahdol (now Anuppur) district in eastern Madhya Pradesh. There, with his close friend and helpmate Shamrao, he set up his 'ashram', named after St. Francis of Assisi, hoping to propagate the saint's ideals and beliefs amidst the forests, ridges and spurs of the Maikal hills, close to where the holy Narmada river had its source. Living in a mud-and-thatch hut like the local Gond tribals, the two started a small dispensary, a school, a tailoring and carpentry section to teach both crafts and self-reliance, and a leper rehabilitation centre. Eight smaller 'ashrams' were also set up, which worked as extensions of the main ashram and at one point of time there were nearly four hundred children studying, mostly from the Gond and other neighbouring tribes. His Christian values of justice and humanism now mingled with his growing commitment through selfless service to the needy, the exploited and the dispossessed.

According to the autobiography, Elwin was kept under scrutiny by both the British administration and the senior clergy and had had several brushes with both. He fell foul of the then Bishop of Nagpur on allegations that he was promoting the Congress party and its nationalist ideology through his activities as he failed to swear allegiance to the King-Emperor. This tussle went on till about 1935 when he left the Church of England. He had to undergo further humiliation by having to sign a Deed of Relinquishment in 1936 under the Clerical Disabilities Act 1870 of the UK, to be able to come back to India and continue serving (he had gone on a short visit to England to meet his mother). In the same year, he moved his ashram to Sanhrwachhappar, a further 18 kilometres or so to the south of Karanjia, where he continued to work amongst the Gond, Raj Gond, Mehera and the Agaria tribes. It was here that he became immersed in his twin passions of service and scholarship. In 1935, his first book (written jointly with Shamrao Hivale) entitled Songs of the Forest:

*The Folk Poetry of the Gonds* was published by Allen and Unwin. Now, he became increasingly involved with research and writing, bringing out a sort of annotated diary, *Leaves from the Jungle* in 1936, and two novels depicting the life of the tribals as he had witnessed it at Karanjia and Sanhrwachhappar, with the *Phulmat of the Hills* in 1937 and the *Cloud that's Dragonish* in 1938. This was followed by his masterly monograph entitled *The Baiga* in 1939.

In 1940, he moved once again, this time to Patangarh, in the Dindori *tehsil* of the then Central Provinces (now Madhya Pradesh) but closer to the Narmada river, among the local Baiga and Pardhan tribes. He was already deeply interested in and involved with collecting data and trying to understand the local folklore and folk cultures. His sense of identification with the local tribals grew when in the same year he married Kosi, a Gond lady. Unfortunately, this marriage did not last, and around 1949 (as later information showed), he divorced Kosi and married Lila, a Pardhan lady, and thereafter enjoyed a happy and contented family life. While, as Elwin himself mentions, Shamrao looked after the day to day work of the dispensary, school and leper treatment, he increasingly devoted more time to studies and to writing that would quickly develop into his more formal anthropological researches into the tribes of India. It was at about this time in 1940, that he went to Bastar and started work there as Census Officer of the state and commenced his researches into the Bison-horn Maria and the Muria of the area. In 1942, he visited some of the tribal areas of central Orissa, particularly among the Juangs of Bonai, Pal Lahara and Keonjhar, following which he was appointed Honorary Anthropologist to the Orissa Government. In the meantime, he had been writing and publishing his monographs, *The Agaria* in 1942 and *Maria Murder and Suicide* in 1943. The compilation *Folk-tales of Mahakoshal* came out in 1944. This was quickly followed by the *Folksongs of Maikal Hills*, a compilation of folksongs of the Gond, Baiga, the Pardhan, and other local tribes in 1944 and *Folksongs of Chhattisgarh* in 1946, both jointly with Shamrao. In 1946, Elwin was appointed Deputy Director of the Department of Anthropology (as the Anthropological Survey of India was then known) under Dr. B.S. Guha (whose immense contributions to physical anthropology in India had been recorded in the *Ethnographic Notes* by Dr. J.H. Hutton in the Census of India, 1931). This meant moving to Calcutta (where he stayed at 64 Park Street) far from his beloved Patangarh, in the middle of files and official procedures, but he managed to make several visits to the Saora and Bondo tribal areas in Orissa. Elwin was writing prolifically in those years and his magnum opus on the Muria, *Muria and their Ghotul*, was published in 1947, besides numerous other articles and papers. He, however, left the Anthropological Department in 1949 to devote more time to research and writing.

Elwin's first visit to northeast India (where he was to devote his later years) was in 1947, apparently at the invitation of W.G. Archer of the Indian Civil Service, and Elwin's good friend, who was working there briefly. In 1953, he was appointed Anthropological Consultant and thereafter, Adviser on Tribal Affairs to the Government of India, due to which followed another five years of strenuous touring of the tribal areas in Manipur, Nagaland and North Eastern Frontier Agency (NEFA, later Arunachal Pradesh), often on foot for weeks on end through leech-infested forests. He became directly involved, together with N.K. Rustamji of the Indian Civil Service with the selection and training of the Indian Frontier Administration Service officers and in developing a 'Philosophy for NEFA', which was in truth a charter for the development of the tribal areas of India. In the middle of all this, he continued to write, first, another important monograph, the *Bondo Highlander* in 1950, *The Tribal Art of Middle India: A Personal Record* in 1951, *The Tribal Myths of Orissa* in 1954, and another masterly monograph, *The Religion of an Indian Tribe* in 1955.

Elwin had, by then, settled down permanently in Shillong (now the capital of the state of Meghalaya) at the house 'Shridham' in Nongthymmai, and began to put together his collection of tribal artefacts and photographs besides devoting more time to his family. But this relatively more comfortable and sedate life was not to be. He suffered a mild heart attack in 1961 and had to be placed under a more controlled dietary and medical regime. In spite of these restrictions, he chaired the Committee on the Special Multi-purpose Tribal Blocks, involving considerable travelling, and served as a member of the Dhebar Commission on Indian Scheduled Tribes and Castes and wrote the major part of its 600-page report. He suffered another massive heart attack while on a visit to Delhi and passed away on 23 February 1964, even while his autobiography, *The Tribal World of Verrier Elwin* was under print by the Oxford University Press.

Many honours had come the way of this remarkable person, not the least of which were his close contacts with Mahatma Gandhi and Jawaharlal Nehru, and indeed many stalwarts of the Congress Party of those days, notably Vallabhbhai Patel and Jamnalal Bajaj (as mentioned earlier), Bhulabhai Desai, Acharya Kripalani, B.G. Kher and others. He received the Doctorate in 1944 from Oxford and became the Editor of *Man in India* from 1942-48. As I found out later, he was honoured with the S.C. Roy Medal in 1945, and the Annandale Medal in 1951 by the Asiatic Society in Calcutta, the Campbell Medal by the Asiatic Society of Bombay in 1947, was also elected Fellow of the Royal Asiatic Society of Bengal in 1947, and received the Rivers Medal in 1948 of the Royal Anthropological Institute. Possibly, he himself most treasured the grant of Indian citizenship in 1954 and, to an extent, the conferment of Padma Bhushan by the Government of India in 1961.

My reading of *The Tribal World* in 1965 was followed in succession by the *Kingdom of the Young* (an abridged version of his later book, *The Muria and Their Ghotul), Maria Murder and Suicide, Bondo Highlander, Tribal Art of Middle India* and *Leaves from the Jungle* which I either bought or borrowed from the Asiatic Society of which I had become a member by then. Each of these books rang with Elwin's patent sensitivity, his humanism, vast knowledge and capability of sheer physical hardship. Time and again the words and pictures were seen – indeed, scrutinised – and slowly a vague idea of Elwin's India began to take shape. This was far beyond anything a Tourist Bureau pamphlet could say or a casual traveller inform. I travelled in my mind over and over again, over the same forest roads, the wooded hills, across sandy streams, passing laughing people on the way to the local *bazaar,* till they became a part of what I was. His wide-ranging research into Maria suicide, the *ghotul-* practice of the Muria, the religion of the Saora tribe and the descriptions of the lives of the Juang and the Bondo, his monumental compilations of the folksongs and folklore of the tribes of central India, frightened me by their very range and depth. Was it really possible for one man to have accomplished so much?

It was however the picture of the life of the Muria, the Saora, the Juang and of course, Elwin's original fascination – the Baiga – that gripped me totally. I had become familiar with the Santhal people during my annual childhood vacations to Santiniketan (in Birbhum, West Bengal), their ebony skin shining with health, the men stocky with wise, ever-smiling eyes, the women with their hair drawn taut and tied in a knot behind their head, lissome, with a gait and carriage that was the envy of their city-bred sisters. I also used to visit their lovely clean villages in the neighbourhood, see their beautiful measured dances and had occasionally picked up some of their handicrafts of silver and beads. What I now read in *The Tribal World* was something different. It was as if a window overlooking a completely new and strange world had opened up. I ran through *The Tribal World* more than once, and the hum-drum routine of a middle-class college student's life of coffee house '*addas*', I.M.D. Little, Samuelson and the frequent visits to the cinema that I had carefully built up, was shaken to its roots. A new poison – or was it elixir – had entered my veins and over the next twenty years, a fever or haze pulsed through anything and everything that I did or thought of. Elwin had been able to bring out something quite alien to whatever I had so far known or seen, something more elemental, with an umbilical chord tied strongly to the hills and forests, to nature herself. I dreamt not of any dream jobs or climbing some great mountain, but of Sanhrwachhapper in the Maikal Hills and of the Baiga medicine-man, of Keskal *ghats* and the Muria *chelik* and *motiari*, the Kuttia Khond, the country of the Bondo by the turbulent Machkund river, of Parlakimedi and the Saora *kuranboi*, and the great Karma and Marhai dances. There was an inexplicable desperation to see and experience at first hand the tribal world of central India that Elwin had written of. Those five years between 1965, when I first read *The Tribal World Of Verrier Elwin*, and my first journey in 1970 into the unknown had been agonising, with the realisation that time was slipping through my hands and that with every passing month and year, the magical land he had described of the Muria and Maria and the Baiga, was receding farther and farther away. There could be no greater torture than the denial of something so desperately craved. I know. I have suffered.

# 2

# The First Foray

In those days, still some twenty years before personal computers and another five years before the Internet and 'Google Earth', the only source of information was in books or by word of mouth. There was nothing I could gather about Bastar, save what Elwin had written in *The Tribal World*. It was one thing that he had written of Jagdalpur and Kondagaon in Bastar and quite another to locate it more precisely and work out how to actually reach there. All the people whom I asked shook their heads solemnly – no, they had no idea where it was. Moreover, they were not even interested. It was as if the place was not in India and perhaps existed in another world (which in a sense it did, as I subsequently found out). There was a complete 'black-out' of information and it was as if the other world of Elwin had entered into a conspiratorial silence. Then things happened in a rush. My membership to the Asiatic Society in 1968 opened up a huge vista of knowledge and I quickly read up most of Elwin's other books such as *The Baiga, Maria Murder and Suicide, The Muria and Their Ghotul* and bought myself a copy of *Leaves from the Jungle*. Then, later that same year – fortuitously - on a rail journey back from Bombay to visit my sister, I heard the magic word 'Jagdalpur' uttered by a travelling salesman – he said that he would be getting off at Raipur and would catch a bus from there to Jagdalpur, a place mentioned in Elwin's book. Shortly afterwards, a tourist map on central India, of a series that Burmah Shell had published, also came into my hands at a petrol pump. This showed the thick red lines of the national highways, the black lines of the railway, and the thin red lines of the state highways creeping across the map, along with dotted lines of the fair-weather roads, and the swathes of green to denote forests. It also showed Raipur and Jagdalpur, and the tenuous thin lines that connected them and Vizianagram. The map was presumptuous enough to indicate that buses plied over certain highways and roads. This was the first indication I had that people actually lived in that area, communicated with one another, went to markets to haggle over the price of cloth and lived a life, and not what had seemed to be a totally impenetrable void. Then, in 1970, I came across the route map of the Automobile Association of Eastern India with details such as 'IB', 'DB', 'RS', 'ROL, 'ROR' etc., which filled in some of the gaps in my information. It showed highway No. 43 climbing from the plains of Vizianagram, cutting through the ridges and spurs of the Eastern Ghats on the way to Jeypore and after touching Jagdalpur, reaching the hot and dusty town of Raipur on the BNR line in a final burst of speed. So there I was that winter afternoon in 1970 in Vizianagram, taking a chance on the way back from another world of the temples of Kumbhakonam and Kanchipuram in south India, into this 'other world' that Verrier Elwin had written of in his autobiography.

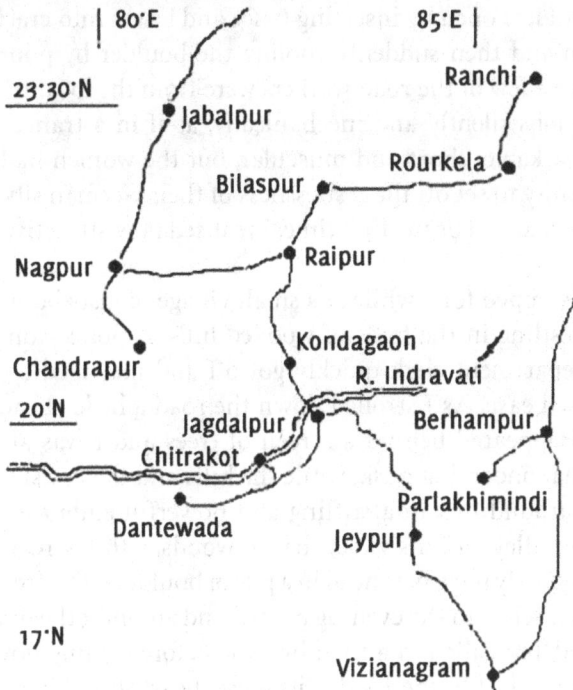

Area of travels by author in central India, 1970 to 1984

The bus creeping through the Eastern Ghats, crossing rivers over shallow causeways, rumbling across rugged streams, passing unknown hamlets, provided a capsule of communication and commerce with the bustling world outside. It snarled its way along the twelve feet wide tarmac, pushing bullock-carts aside, throwing chickens into a frenzy and making people draw up their legs in alarm as they sat on the benches in the wayside stalls having their afternoon tea or snacks. The earth was reddish brown, with patches of open rice fields and stretches of dark and heavy forest. People could be seen working in the fields, appearing as dots in the distance. The occasional herds of cow and buffalo were scattered like black and white carrom counters against the green vegetation. Deep *khuds* appeared, now on the left of the road, now on the right, as the bus climbed the winding road up the hills, while down below narrow streams glistened like a snail's trail in the valleys. Towering over the road, craggy peaks, wrinkled and knobbled, crowded around in sullen silence, watchful. Here and there road gangs could be seen working, splitting the huge boulders open by inserting twigs and leaves into cracks, setting fire to them and then suddenly cooling the boulder by pouring water over it. Quite a few of the road workers were from the local tribes, going about their jobs silently and mechanically, as if in a trance. The men were unremarkable, short and muscular, but the women had a certain grace, a serenity to set off the restlessness of their German silver bangles and bead necklaces. For the first time, I realised how attractive dark skin could be.

The bus stopped for a while at a small village of just about five or six hutments nestling in the folds of wooded hills. A police constable and an excise department clerk quickly got off and managed a cup of tea with practised ease. As I strolled down the road a little ahead, the huts suddenly disappeared behind a screen of trees and I was alone in the middle of that oncoming dusk, while the hills and the forest murmured and closed around me, in a stifling and powerful embrace. Far down below in the valley with its violet shaded woods, a thin stream emerged briefly and quickly buried its head in a pile of boulders. The trees wrestled amongst themselves in the evening breeze, and amongst the branches the birds cackled and called in a final hysteria before settling down for the night. The bus, deaf to these calls, its diesel heart throbbing amidst the stillness of the hills, moved on.

At about seven o'clock in the evening the bus stopped at Sunabeda, one of the newly developing centres in Koraput. Should I get down here for the night? The habitation looked so inviting. The question kept buzzing in my mind, but I decided to press on and got an extension of my bus ticket up to Jeypore, which was, in those days, the headquarters of Koraput district in south western Orissa. The bus rolled into Jeypore bus station at about nine in the night, and relying on an aging *rickshaw-walla*, I allowed myself to be quickly bundled into a lodging for a royal nightly charge of Rs. 4/- only. After a quick meal at a ubiquitous Punjabi hotel, I stretched out on the twin bed eager to face the morning.

Early next morning, I reached the bus stand and was gratified to hear that a bus would be leaving within the hour for Jagdalpur. So, after a hurried breakfast, I boarded the bus dizzy with expectations. The bus turned its face west on national highway 43 towards Jagdalpur. Here, the countryside was more open and dusty, in places smudged grey with clusters of huts, dingy and squalid. There were no more dispersed hutments, the sense of space and stretching that I had left behind in the hills. After some distance, some *adivasi* women boarded the bus, taking their produce to the Jagdalpur market. Their hair in a bun drawn up tight from the forehead and pushed to one side of the neck, a thin chain of gold around the slender neck, quick, animated eyes, tawny brown skin burnished with a rub-down of *mahua* oil were my first impressions. Even if I had not arrived, it seemed that I was at least on my way.

One look at the linen at one of the three rest houses (and it wasn't much of a choice) then functioning in Jagdalpur and it was not difficult to make up my mind that I would rather sleep on my feet than lie down on that bed. Still, a wash-up and a cup of tea helped to lighten my mood and I went off mingling with the local people, *adivasis* mostly, who were on their way to the local market, carrying baskets slung on bamboo poles across their shoulder that danced at every step they took. I followed the stream of people, past the *bania* with their bolts of cheap cloth, German silver ornaments and bangles, aluminium utensils, pan shops, a small and unkempt State Bank of India branch office and there, on the left and a little distance off in a large field, was the market. It was a market and a funfair combined in full swing. A great babble of voices bargaining, buying, selling, arguing was heard and the dust churned up by hundreds of human feet and cattle rose in ochre billows between the clumps of mango trees bordering the market place. Squatting here and there were wizened old men with scruffy salt and pepper whiskers, with a short *dhoti* wound tightly around their loins and a small *shawl* around their shoulders completing their attire. They sat patiently on their haunches, chatting at ease with friends and neighbours, in a low murmur, occasionally with a small gesture of the hand to emphasise a point, with all the dignity of a Roman senator. The younger men were in the middle with their ware of plaited cattle ropes, an array of clay utensils, wooden drums, bunches of tendu leaves spread out, trying to catch the eye of prospective customers with a wave of the hand, shouting and jostling one and another. To one side, there were about five cane crushers turned by scrawny buffaloes squeezing out small trickles of juice from thin sugarcane stalks - five *paise* for a glassfull. On the edge of the road, bullock carts, one side down like seesaws, stood in a row, while mothers cooked over small fires with their babies cocooned in a cloth sling around their shoulders. The young bucks joked amongst themselves showing off their skill with the drums, calling each other names and eyeing the girls clustered here and there under the scattered shadows of the mango trees. On the other side of the field, the Poroja and other *adivasi* traded their fresh vegetables, potatoes and onions, sharing the honour with *mahua* flowers, tamarind pods and dried fish in round wicker baskets. Here and there hawkers selling coloured ribbons and pins, combs and mirrors mingled with some *banias* selling kerosene, rice, bolts of cloth or cheap ready-made garments and German silver ware. Respectable housewives, servants, *adivasi* women talked, shouted, gesticulated and snatched at these few moments of change in the daily routine of their life to see something fresh and reach out across the pale distance of illiteracy and untouchability. Like so many flowers, the young girls in red and yellow bordered white saris or in bright ochre cloth flitted about, arms around each others shoulders, the head lowered as much to protect the face from cruel glances as to save the bucks from being pierced by the sparkle of their eye, the sudden gleam of a smile; supple, dark and beautiful. In the middle of all this, I felt completely like an outsider, an interloper, with my baggy jeans from New Market, Trumoc shoes from Bata, a Swiss made wristwatch and a Kodak Brownie camera. In this festival of colours, of unselfconscious gaiety, of unexpected laughter and tears, of short *dhotis* and equally short *saris*, I was a total outsider, self-conscious, embarrassed and anxious.

Even my spectacles stood out. It was remarkable how few people wore spectacles in this area. I saw only one old *bania* with round steel framed spectacles tied with a string over his ears. I roamed the market ground, I do not know for how long, not really seeing the people but absorbing through my nose, ears and eyes the slightly sweaty tang of the dust, the bell-like laughter and the kaleidoscopic play of red, yellow, white and tawny brown, as if intoxicated. After some time I hurried away, fearing that I would be overwhelmed by the sights and sounds of that enchanted market place.

'Chitrakot?' asked the owner of the restaurant, proudly named Royal Punjab Hotel, loath to be drawn away from scribbling orders for *dal ka tarka* and *alu gobi*, apparently quite innocent of the South Eastern Railways publicity poster at Esplanade that had mentioned Chitrakot as one of the most picturesque waterfalls in Central India. What was perhaps more important for me was that it was at Chitrakot that Elwin had first set up camp in Bastar when he arrived to study the tribes, the Maria and Muria of Bastar. In Elwin's days, Bastar was still an independent kingdom at least nominally ruled by the descendants of the Kakatiya dynasty, a branch of the kings who had once ruled in Warangal, in adjoining Andhra Pradesh. They had been driven off by Muslim invaders sometime in the fifteenth century and had sought refuge amidst the hills and jungles of Bastar across the Godavari river. Like so many other kingdoms in India, Bastar was largely under the supervision of a Resident Agent or Administrator of the British Government in India or by the District Collector appointed by them. Elwin had first been invited by W.V. Grigson of the Indian Civil Service, who had been the District Collector of Bastar from 1927 to 1931, to set up an establishment there and also to take up a study of the local tribals (Elwin was to do considerable work on the Baiga and the Agaria *adivasis* near Patangarh). Wilfred Grigson was equally interested in ethnology and had written the book *Maria Gonds of Bastar* (published by Oxford University Press, 1938). However, Elwin had not been able to make it then and it was only in 1940 that he was able to act upon the fresh invitation of A.N. Mitchell, the then Administrator, with the added attraction of the prospect of being the Census Officer in Bastar.

A hawker at the bus stand was a little more helpful and said that a private bus shuttled between Jagadalpur and Chitrakot every day, going out in the evening and coming back to the town the next day after an overnight halt at Chitrakot. In Elwin's days, of course, such a bus did not exist but he has written that in fair weather most of the roads were motorable. My watch read about two-thirty in the afternoon and after a hasty tea and wrapping together a couple of *chapattis* and some dry vegetable curry, I was soon on the private bus, which I found was more like a pick-up van, a wooden cage with a couple of rickety seats built on an old truck chasis. Not unexpectedly, the driver was a grizzled old Sikh with his pyjama strings hanging almost to his knees. The bus started off at four-thirty but halted every 50 or 100 yards on the westbound road linking Jagdalpur to Gidam picking up stragglers who had come to the Jagdalpur weekly *bazaar* and were now on their way home at the corner of some distant field. Quickly enough, the bus became full of people huddled close to each other, knees interlocked and toes stacked on top of one another, with a sweet-sour all-pervading smell of sweat and country liquor. Struggling with its load of humanity, the bus sputtered and gasped across a wide plateau, patterned with rice fields, and after a while, with stretches of dense sal forests. One by one bidding farewell, the travellers got off in stages till the driver, the conductor and myself were the only people left. It was already quite dark when with a sudden screech, the bus swerved sharply and stopped with a jolt, and the Sardar jumped out from his cabin shouting '*pakro… pakro*'. I thought that either we had been attacked by some miscreants or had run over some person. With much gusto our Sardar explained that he had tried to run over a rabbit that had dashed across the road. Finally, without further excitement, the bus ran on through the deepening evening for another three or four miles, till it went off the road, and with a U-turn came to a stop at a clearing. We had reached Chitrakot. A short distance away, one could hear the roar of the river as it found itself tumbling head over heels over a cliff. The bus had stopped near an old Siva temple and in the court-yard three sadhus had lit a fire and, apparently high on liquor or *hashish*, were chanting something and occasionally shaking the iron spike they carried with themselves, making the rings at the end of the spike jangle sharply. Somewhat put off by the lack of warm welcome and not a little apprehensive of the three sadhus with their matted hair piled high on their head, ash-smeared body and bursts of chanting, I turned to the conductor to ask where they would be putting up for the night. He said that they were going to sleep the night in the bus and when I asked if I could join – there being safety in numbers - he sounded somewhat taken aback and wanted to know why I should want to do that when there was a rest house nearby. Curiosity and pride prevailed and I allowed myself to be led away from the sanctuary of the bus for about 100 yards off through a thicket till a small bungalow with a large verandah came into view. Our shouts for the *chowkidar* yielded, after a few minutes, a short stocky person, obviously not too happy to have been woken up from a dreamless sleep. He apparently did not know much Hindi, but with some frantic sign language he was made to understand that I wanted to put up at the rest house and would he please try to get me some food. I was left waiting on the verandah with my bag while the *chowkidar* went for a lantern and keys, and the river roared on endlessly nearby. Overhead, the stars scattered like fireflies across the sky that curved like an immense inverted bowl of the deepest velvet black. There was nobody around, not for about four or five miles, apart from the three sadhus whose chants could be faintly heard, the bus driver and the conductor (now no doubt fast asleep) and the *chowkidar*. With a rattle and a creak, the door of one of the rooms was opened and with grunts and signals I was led in. Before the *chowkidar* vanished into the darkness, I tried once more with sign language ask for food and water. But to no avail, for he signalled with a sad shake of his head that no food was available but he would get me a jar of water. Out of necessity, I fell back on the two *chapattis* and vegetables I had brought as emergency rations and in spite of being cold and leathery, they took the edge off my hunger. I had to get into bed fully dressed as the night was biting cold with a rising wind that rattled at the doors and made the windows creak ominously. With all this and remembering the wild-looking sadhus, sleep took a long time to come.

The next morning saw me up with the sun and outside on the fields bordering the gorge, through which the Indravati river plunged magnificently as the Chitrakot falls. The drop was about 150 feet, but more than that, the wide, crescent shaped lip of the fall brought the river down with a great roar as the mist billowed up through the cold morning. It was bigger, much bigger, than the Hudru and Jona falls near Ranchi that I had seen in my childhood. More importantly, as far as I could see, across the river stretched a mess of hills, ridges and spurs clothed in deep dark forests. This, I knew, was Abujhmarh, the home of the Hill Maria, the very heart of Bastar. A rainbow leapt out of the gorge to greet the sun but my eyes and heart were turned towards the hills that beckoned mysteriously from across the river. The cold, chilly morning air formed a cold column inside my chest, as I tried to breathe in the rough and broken plateau, the clumps of sal, the water hurtling down the gorge and the gentle curving of the river beyond the rapids, and the dead silence all around pierced only by the roar of the falls. Back at the bungalow, tea was held up as a man had been sent to another village about three miles away to get some milk for the tea. It was not till about seven-thirty that our man arrived with enough milk, which barely filled half a cigarette tin, but that was enough for a couple of cups of tea. A few sweet potatoes baked over wood fire washed down by the tea was my breakfast and we were soon on the way back to Jagdalpur.

My next destination was Narainpur, also written of in Elwin's books. This time the bus stand hawker was hardly any more informative than the restaurant owner, but asking around some of the bus drivers got me the information about the next bus to Kondagaon. This, I had learnt from a study of the maps and from Elwin's books, was the main road-head for Narainpur, which in turn was the main staging point for Abujhmarh and the country of the Muria and Hill Maria. Once more I had a hurried lunch and was on a bus riding through sun-lit plains, past villagers hurrying home before the evening came on, huts scattered randomly and looking tiny below the spreading mango and tamarind trees. We reached Kondagaon as evening fell, where the people looked tired at the end of their day; the constable sitting slackly at the local *thana*, the hawkers gathering up their wares before returning home, the tea-shop owner heating up the brew one last time before he also downed shutters. One by one, the petromax lanterns and the occasional electric bulb came on, casting pale squares of light around the bus stand. Questions as to when the next bus to Narainpur would leave were answered with a vague wave of the hand; sometimes maybe this evening or maybe tomorrow. Time, as we understand and value it, just did not seem to matter. While I was ruefully brooding over the possibility of having to spend the night at the bus stand, and taking the next bus to Raipur and from there take the quickest possible train back to Calcutta, perhaps never ever to come back, a lean and short person with shining eyes and flashing white teeth spoke up from the shadows next to the bus stand. He said that he too would be going to Narainpur and would take me along. I had no means of knowing whether he would cut my throat in the process or merely relieve me of my purse. But somehow, I felt that he was a good person and wanted to do good for a stranded traveller. He introduced himself as M.R. Singh, an assistant in the District Industries Department who was required to travel considerably up and down the district and was now stationed at Narainpur. He was thrilled to know that I had recently been as far down as Kanyakumari and Rameswaram, and repeatedly said how fortunate he was to have met a person who had been to these holy places. So, shortly afterwards, the true-to-type ramshackle bus turned up and somehow, Singh and I managed to scrambled aboard. The weak headlights of the bus marked out the crizzled trunks of sal and mango trees lining the road, the occasional meandering streams, and the very occasional small huts. The Muria, the men with their short *dhotis*, shoulder length hair and tight white turban on their heads and the womenfolk in their equally short *saris* and baskets of produce on their heads returning home in the evening, scampered away in fear from the oncoming bus, with some even hiding behind trees. Were we to pass only thus, as strangers, I in my time capsule of a bus from Kondagaon with its electricity, banks, people playing cards, and the Muria from their tiny villages in the deep shade of huge mango and tamarind trees? Would I ever be able to see them, the *chelik* and the *motiari*, the Sirdar and Jalyaro, as Elwin had written in his books, so that my fever could cool? Even he had bemoaned more than once that he had begun his studies too late; that the heydays of the tribals, when they were truly the kings of their domain, were well on their way to passing. Only time would tell.

At long last we arrived at Narainpur, with its half a dozen shops lit by petromax lights alongside the bus-stand, about a dozen other houses, half-hidden in the darkness and behind the boles of huge mango trees. Mr. Singh led me to the P.W.D. rest house, where I was very properly shown to the verandah where I could keep my bag and sleep – for official form had to be maintained even in the middle of nowhere. Singh made up for it by kindly escorting me to the Raj Hotel (comprising a counter, four tables, six rickety chairs, and pictures of half a dozen gods and goddesses) run by two brothers from Kerala where I had a quick supper of fairly decent *dosas*.

Next morning, as I strolled out of the rest house on my way to another round of *dosas*, there was Nawab Ali Khan seated by his cycle shop to greet me with a lusty *salaam* as if he knew me for a long time; he did not. I did not even know his name till he introduced himself a couple of minutes later. He was fascinated by the Bengali *Babu* and proudly showed off some pictures of himself and the shop framed next to his low seat. He was only too ready to hire out a cycle to me and I was out cycling within about half an hour.

Narainpur had been a major centre for Elwin's researches in the 1940s into the Muria and their institution of the *ghotul* or adolescent dormitory. Scattered amidst the low hills, with patches of cultivation close to streams and *nullahs* and shaded by clumps of mango, jack fruit and tamarind trees, were the villages that Elwin had written of: Benur, Markabera, Munjhmeta, Bakulwahi, Garh Bangal and others. I had just read about them and this was now the opportunity to see and experience them. As I took the rough road that led off south at a tangent from the Kondagaon-Narainpur road, I could see in the distance the rugged hills of Abujhmarh rising like a dragon's spine, hazy with thick forests. I passed the occasional Muria carrying an axe with the blade shaped somewhat like a shepherd's crook so that it hung easily from the shoulder without having to be held in the hand. *Dhoti* tied tightly around the waist, a hard, wiry physique, German silver bangles on the wrist, brass earrings and either a tight white turban or bare headed with the hair shaved back to the line of the ears and tied with a knot at the nape of the neck. All around there were clumps of gigantic mango trees, tamarind and sal casting their soft inviting shade. Branching off on the right towards the blue hills, I went across a couple of hill streams, sand-bedded with rough grass fringing their banks. To the right, nestling amongst the mango and tamarind was a tribal village that looked as if it had been painted against the green. Pushing the cycle before me, I threaded my way through the shrubbery towards the huts. On the left, near a threshing ground, hanging from a hay-loft, was a string instrument carved with a wide-hipped bowl at the bottom, covered with a speckled lizard's skin, a slim and long waist, and three keys standing out like ears. For me, this was the first tribal musical instrument that I had ever come across and it seemed as if it had been fashioned from the soul of a man, covered with the skin of a dragon and strung with the tail spume of the flying horse. I asked an *adivasi* boy standing near the threshing floor if he would sell it. No, he shook his head, it belonged to his brother and no, he did not know when he would return or would at all like to sell it. Two rupees, five rupees (which was a good deal of money in 1970) but Bilku, for that was his name he said, who possibly never had 8 annas to his name, would hear nothing of it. This taught me, again for the first time that, as with the concept of time, money was not a major consideration in most parts of tribal India, and that music and songs, that intrinsic part of their life and culture, could not be bought and sold but could be gifted out of affection and friendship.

That afternoon I returned to Kondagaon and even with this brief three day visit, it was as if I was leaving something of myself behind and not even the later rough and tumble for the night express bus ticket to Raipur and the falling at the feet of the reservation clerk for a reserved sleeper berth (for it would still take another fifteen years for the introduction of computerised train reservations) to Calcutta, could make me forget or make me whole again.

# 3

# Through Elwin's Eyes

Imagine a district that was once (now split up into several units following substantial re-organisation) about fourteen thousand square miles in size, or about as large as the state of Kerala, set a short distance below the South-Eastern Railway line running between Calcutta and Bombay, practically plumb in the middle of India. The district stretched from the Keskal *ghats* in the north to Konta on the banks of the Godavari river in the south, and from somewhere near Jeypore in the Koraput district of Orissa in the east, to the Pranhita river bordering Chanda in Maharasthtra to the west. After the Chhattisgarh plains, that range from Bilaspur in the east, Kawardha in the north to Rajnandgaon to the west come to a halt at the foot of the Keskal *ghats*, the land rises to a high, undulating plateau, deeply broken by a great mass of hills and ridges that constitute Abujhmarh practically at the centre of the district, and again in the south, around the Bailadila hills. This land is a huge melting pot of tribes of south-central India – the Muria, Maria, Dhurwa, Dorla, Bhattra, Poroja and a medley of associated castes such as the Lohar, Kumhar, the Gharwa and others. For the record, in the parlance of physical anthropology, these people are largely Dravidian in features and language (with some elements of the proto-Australoid in some areas), with considerable infusion of the Gonds who may have immigrated centuries ago from farther north.

That Elwin came to love this area is evident from the introductory lines in *The Muria and Their Ghotul*, which are as notable as a literary piece as a description of the local geography. As with many other regions of India, the rivers with their changing moods and impetuosity define and add character to Bastar. The principal river is the Indravati, which races down from its source in the hills of Kalahandi in Orissa, lying to the east, and cuts almost through the centre of the district, before leaping over the Chitrakot falls (lying almost at the centre point of Bastar), and then runs over rock-gird rapids and deep pools to its confluence with the Godavari, close to Bhopalpatnam, far to the west. The other important rivers that thread through the hills and forests of Bastar are the Baordigh, the Gudra, the Nibra and the Kotri (the latter two draining the Abujhmarh) which fall into the Indravati from the north and the Sankini-Dankini, with their alternating dark-red and jade green waters, from the south. The vast stretches of forest that Elwin described are more to be seen during and after the monsoon rains, for the forest is largely of the dry deciduous type, though with extensive patches of sal, which shed their leaves with the onset of winter and look green and full for the better part of the summer. It is, however, to Grigson (as given in his *Maria Gonds of Bastar*) that we have to turn for the masterly account of the history and geography of Bastar (as admitted by Elwin himself). Grigson also noted that motorable roads (at least in fair weather) had come up even by that time connecting Narainpur to Orchha in Abujhmarh, Tirathgarh to Dantewada (in the Bison-horn Maria country) via Katakalyan and Kuakonda, besides the main road from Jagdalpur westwards to Bhopalpatnam (almost on the Chanda border of Maharashtra) via Gidam and Bijapur. These were used to an extent by Elwin during his subsequent travels in Bastar.

Into this wild country of hills and forests came an off-shoot of the famous Kakatiya dynasty of Warangal in Andhra Pradesh (who had ruled there between 1150 to about 1425 AD), driven off by the depredations of Ahmed Shah Bahmani. But this was not the only or the first thrust by non-tribals – historical records suggest that there had been several raids as early as 894 and 1100 AD by the elements of the Eastern and the Western Chalukya, and later by the Chola and Hoysala princes. These, however, largely confined themselves to the valley of the Indravati river and its adjoining areas, as the archaeological remains at Kuruspal, Barsur, Dantewada and Bhairamgarh villages (all confined to the central area of Bastar) indicate. As if that was not enough, in the early nineteenth century, Maratha forces under the intrepid Niloo Pandit came down from the north but were repulsed near the village of Bastar, which stands near Jagdalpur on the Jagdalpur-Raipur highway. The tussle, however, continued for many years and the Maratha influence increased till the

British established their administration over that region. For all practical purposes, the Kakatiya dynasty had gone into decline since a rebellion during the reign of Rudra Pratap around 1910. The reign of Prafulla Kumari Devi around 1924 practically brought the curtain down on the Kakatiya dynasty in Bastar; although the king nominally continued to rule, albeit under the watchful eye of the British and then the Indian government. Even this façade of masterly inaction was rudely shattered when Praveen Chandra Bhanj Deo, the king of Bastar, was killed during a skirmish with the state police in 1964.

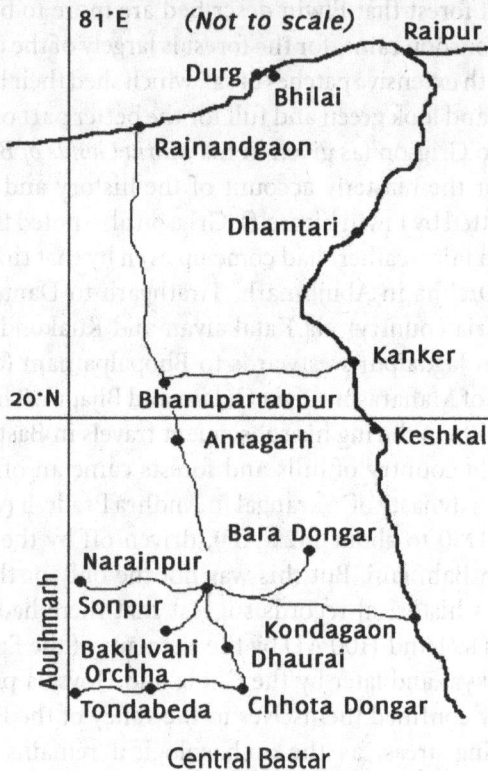

81°E     (Not to scale)     Raipur

Durg
    Bhilai
Rajnandgaon
        Dhamtari
                Kanker
20°N   Bhanupartabpur
    Antagarh     Keshkal
        Bara Dongar
Narainpur
Sonpur
        Kondagaon
Bakulvahi   Dhaurai
Orchha
Tondabeda   Chhota Dongar

Abujhmarh

Central Bastar

Elwin had been informed sometime around 1934 or 1935 about Bastar by W.V. Grigson. A word about Grigson himself – he was about six years older than Elwin and had had his education in the Classics at Christ Church College in Oxford. Since joining the service in 1919, he had served in many capacities in the Central Provinces, rising to be the

Secretary to the Governor of the Central Provinces and Berar in 1941, and later as Minister of Revenue, Backward Classes, Town and Country Planning in 1946, before retiring in 1947, when he moved to Pakistan; he died in 1948. He was more than happy to extend whatever information and assistance possible to a fellow-Oxonian, Elwin. His book *The Maria Gonds of Bastar* (originally published in 1938 and re-published in 1949) was seminal in content and it is possible that his other publications *The Aboriginal Problem in Central Provinces and Berar*, 1944, and *The Aboriginal in the Future India*, 1945, would have been found useful later by Elwin, who in fact acknowledges in *The Muria and Their Ghotul* the use of some unpublished notes by Grigson.

As indicated by Elwin in the Preface to his book, *Maria Murder and Suicide* (1943), he had visited Bastar several times between 1935 and 1940, when Mr. E.S. Hyde, ICS, was in charge of Bastar. It was, however, not till early 1940 that Elwin was able to get away from his responsibilities in Patangarh and spend some months continuously there. He had already published several essays and monographs by then, most notably the *Songs of the Forest* (1935, jointly with Shamrao Hivale), *Leaves from the Jungle* (1936), *Phulmat of the Hills* (1937) and followed in 1939 with his extensive monograph, *The Baiga*. He was already putting the finishing touches to another notable monograph, *The Agaria* (published in 1942) on the *adivasi* community, who produce iron by an ancient process, mostly in south-eastern and south central areas of the country. Thus, he had been able to reach out to the eyes and minds of people quite at a distance from his *ashram* in Patangarh and to some in positions of authority, notably W.V. Grigson, J.H. Hutton (author of The *Sema Nagas* and editor of the notable ethnographic section in the Census of India Report 1931), and W.G. Archer, all of the Indian Civil Service. Despite the work of E.H. Dalton and W.W. Hunter in the nineteenth century (more in the nature of compilations rather than field research), and some sporadic ethnographic notes by a few civil and police officials till the mid-1930s, there had only been the work of Sarat Chandra Roy on the Munda and Oraon of Ranchi and J.P. Mills and J.H. Hutton on the Nagas of north-east India. However, official interest in ethnography and anthropology was growing as evidenced by the extensive ethnographic notes appended by J.H. Hutton to the Census Report of 1931, together with a major contribution on physical anthropology by B.S. Guha.

However, the undertaking of field research on ethnography or cultural anthropology was still quite limited, certainly with respect to the tribes of south-central India. The fact that till 1946 there was no formal Anthropological Survey of India is itself a commentary on the state of ethnographic research in India. It functioned fitfully – and tellingly – as a section in the Zoological Survey of India! However, post-graduate courses in sociology or anthropology had commenced at the Bombay University (where G.S. Ghurye was teaching), at Lucknow with D.N. Majumdar and at the Calcutta University, where Prof. K.P. Chattopadhyay and Prof. Nirmal Kumar Bose were well-known faculty members.

Thus, it came about around this time that Elwin was invited (most possibly on a reference by Grigson or Hutton or both) by A.N. Mitchell, then the Administrator of Bastar, to work as Census Officer of the state. Elwin moved from Patangarh, via Jagdalpur to a village very close to Chitrakot falls – possibly the very same from which the milk had been brought for my morning tea on my previous journey!

He worked there, more or less continuously, till mid 1943, and the results were the two major publications, *Maria Murder and Suicide* in 1943 and *The Muria and Their Ghotul* in 1947. Interestingly enough, the Indravati river forms a sort of natural boundary between the Bison-horn Maria (so-called because of the elaborate bison-horn head-dress they wear on ceremonial occasions) who largely inhabit the southern part of the country, and the Muria who populate the north. The country south of the Indravati is at a lower elevation than that of the northern plateau, and is generally undulating with low hills and wide swathes of relatively flat land where settled cultivation is done. The Bailadila hills are farther to the south and the Tulsidongri hills are away to the east, thus possibly creating a rain-shadow area in-between. The climate of south Bastar is harsh with low rainfall, and high summer temperatures sometimes reaching 48 to 50°C, along with high humidity.

The location of Elwin's village near Chitrakot would have allowed him to visit the Bison-horn Maria villages within about fifty kilometres, besides access to the jails at Jagdalpur and Dantewada where he could find records of homicides and even talk to some of the Maria in detention, to collect data and to understand the phenomenon of the relatively high rate of murder and suicide amongst them. At the same time, he could also make forays into the Muria villages north of Jagdalpur, such as those near Mardapal and Kondagaon. In this he displayed both the eclecticism and the mental discipline that was Elwin's hallmark. He started the simultaneous collection of information and data on both the Maria homicides and the Muria culture, with particular reference to the 'ghotul' of the latter. He was ably assisted in the initial stages by Shamrao Hivale, with his inimitable capability to befriend a tribal and earn his confidence (as admitted by Elwin in more than one place) and later by his wife, Kosi, who being a Gond herself, was also able to relate to the thoughts and beliefs of the Muria and Maria.

Elwin was struck by the high order of differences between the Muria and the Maria with respect to murders and suicides (by a factor of 2.5 to 3). Elwin ascribed this in some part to settled agriculture of the latter, with deep attachment to individual plots of land and its produce. This was exacerbated by strong norms concerning infringements of social behaviour, especially regarding the fidelity and chastity of the spouse. A belief in sorcery, together with gods who demand a high degree of compliance with social practices and customs created a high degree of anxiety and mental tension that may lead to either suicide or murder among the Bison-horn (or the Dandami) Maria. Elwin appreciated that one should approach the problem of the high rate of homicide amongst the Maria from their view-point; for, as he pointed out, what may appear trivial to a visiting official or a court of law, may be in terms of social customs of the Maria, something highly reprehensible. Add to this the free availability of both fermented and distilled liquor and the back-breaking work in the fields to eke out a living in that harsh environment. These make a potent combination which creates a feeling of desperation and sudden outbreaks of rage, often over trivialities, resulting in grievous physical hurt. As the Maria sometimes put it, in the process of killing a person, he often destroyed himself. Elwin took note that confinement in a jail was quite intolerable to the Maria, and they sometimes begged to be hanged instead. Elwin, therefore, pleaded for a more humanitarian approach to the correction of the Maria, such as a type of open camp where he could do some gardening or any other homely activity, and thus recoup his spirit and belief in society and the system.

While Elwin discussed in considerable details the Maria homicides, supported by hard data culled from jail records, he was also able to fill in a great deal of information on the culture and social customs and beliefs of the Maria concerning birth, marriage and death that would have otherwise been lost to posterity. He drew attention to the carved funerary pillars or 'khamba' often built to commemorate some well-known figure amongst the Bison-horn Maria. Some of the festivals such as the Bhimul Pandum, the mango-eating ceremony, the pre-sowing Wijja Pandum festival and the observance of the Dussehra festival were also covered.

Elwin was, however, completely fascinated by the 'ghotul' of the Muria of the northern plateau and hills - the dormitory for young unmarried boys and girls, where they go to spend their night amongst their peers, away from their family hearth. It was not as if such dormitories were unique to the Muria – in earlier years, they were well-known in the hills of Nagaland, and amongst the Munda and Oraon of Ranchi and Hazaribagh. They had also been extensively studied in other parts of the world, such as among the Trobriand Islanders, in New Guinea, in Fiji and elsewhere. While the youth dormitory system had largely declined by 1940s, they existed in the Muria areas of Bastar. This study was undertaken simultaneously with that on the Bison-horn Maria (so much so that in *Maria Murder and Suicide* published in 1943, Elwin found it possible to specifically refer to his forthcoming title, *The Muria and Their Ghotul*, although that came out in print only in 1947). The study area ranged from the Kondagaon *tehsil* lying along and to the east of the main Jagdalpur-Raipur road, to the Narainpur *tehsil* that extended along and to the north and south of the Kondagaon-Narainpur road. Elwin was in his element here, with his powers of observation, interview skills and general facility to interact with tribals, already honed to a fine edge since his Baiga days. He had already been exposed to a set of sexual mores amongst the Baiga of Mandla and Dindori, as may well exist between any two consenting adults, which were quite different – to put it mildly - from what he knew back in the British Isles. To the son of a clergyman, it must have been particularly fascinating that the *ghotul* exemplified the social sanction for a good amount of sexual fore-play, such as petting and fondling and to an extent even pre-marital sex amongst adolescent boys and girls. As Elwin was to find out, such pre-marital relationships were sanctioned between adolescents who had not even been betrothed – and were in fact not even expected to!

Elwin in his works mentioned earlier, supplemented to a considerable extent the more academically-oriented monograph *The Maria Gonds of*

*Bastar* by W.V. Grigson, by giving it a more 'human face' and a fuller description of their day-to-day lives rather than going by the cephalic and nasal indices and study of linguistics. In discussing the *ghotul*, he has not omitted to speak about the clans or *phratries*, or the gods of the Muria, nor indeed about the various types of liquor that they consumed at different ceremonies. The pages of his book resonate with names of the Muria gods, such as Bara Pen, Anga Deo and his children Lalit Kuar, Son Kuar, and those of Bhimulpen, Dulha Deo. But it is the legend of Lingo Pen that was central to the Gond tradition. This legend is a hoary tradition, common - with minor variations - amongst a large section of the tribals inhabiting central India. This was first documented by Rev. Stephen Hislop, then a Missionary of the Free Church of Scotland in Nagpur, and was edited and published in 1866 by Sir Richard Temple, then Chief Commissioner of the Central Provinces. Lingo had a miraculous birth, bursting forth from a flower and drying upon falling on a heap of turmeric – the common cleansing and purifying agent in India. He went hunting with his elder brothers and later cleared the forest and planted rice. He made a musical instrument from a bottle gourd, a bamboo stick and two long strands of hair from his head. Once he started playing on this, the people started dancing. Although he was himself unmarried and spent his time largely playing his musical instruments and dallying with the local maidens, he arranged to get his brother Gonds married off - building a marriage booth of leaves, sprinkling turmeric and tying garlands of flowers – much as Gonds still do to this day. His sisters-in-law, however, became jealous of his attention to the other girls and conspired to seduce Lingo into adultery with them. Lingo was unmoved and rebuffed their overtures (although Hislop has it that he pounded them to good effect with a rice pestle!). The sisters-in-law then complained to their husbands – Lingo's Gond brothers – claiming that Lingo had misbehaved with them. The brothers were incensed on hearing this and decided to kill him while out hunting one day. They failed to kill Lingo, but subjected him to a trial by ordeal to prove his innocence. Lingo passed the ordeal, for he was untainted by any temptations, and went to play with the girls and indulge in his first love, singing and dancing.

While discussing the *ghotul* and its features and functions in Muria society, Elwin has ranged far and wide into the principal myths and beliefs of the Muria, their social organisation and practices, songs and dances, food and common beverages, handicrafts and so on. He has admitted that the attributes of the *ghotul* were not uniform across the areas inhabited by the Muria. Elwin had found that there were basically two types of *ghotuls* in terms of the liberties they permitted for pre-marital sex. One he called '*joridar*', meaning that the respective boys and girls were sort of 'paired' for the period they lived in the *ghotul*, and the other was '*adal badal*', where the partners were changed around either every day or every now and then. Moreover, the villages around Keskal and Antagarh (lying to the north) had been considerably influenced by the Chhattisgarhi people of Rajnandgaon and Durg. Those near Sonpur (to the west of Narainpur) had been under the Maharashtrian influence of Chanda district, while the Hill Maria and their beliefs and practices had affected the villages nestling close to Abujhmarh. But be it north, south, east or west, there were certain features that remained common such as division of the Muria into clans – Elwin with his usual thoroughness identified 34 – such as the Nag, Bagh, Kacchim (or Kashyap), Netam and so on grouped under five broad families. The clan gods were worshipped at certain designated places such as Semurgaon or Tondabeda, although practically every village had its own collection of lesser gods, often the 'sons' or 'nephews' of the principal gods, such as Burha Pen, or Anga Pen, Mata Dei or Danteswari Mai. The marriage ceremonies were also largely similar, with a marriage booth made of branches and leaves, anointment of both the bride and the groom with turmeric, and plenty of drinking and dancing put in for good measure! Elwin described a number of dances such as those around Diwali, or the Pus Kolang in early January, or the Chait in March, the robust and energetic Hulki dances, and so on. There were also several commonly accepted norms concerning permissible marriage partners (to be largely decided by the parents), about adultery and pre-marital pregnancies, taboos during the menses and pregnancies, ritual bathing, etc. After cremating the dead, the ashes are usually kept in an earthen pot, which, after some years, is taken to the place of worship of the clan-god where the pot is broken and sacrifices are made to propitiate the departed and the gods. In the villages close to Abujhmarh, there was also the practice of erecting large stone menhirs in the memory of the dead.

Elwin has discussed several broad aspects as to why such adolescent dormitories at all came up amongst different tribal communities the world over – from a 'trophy room', to a place where future warriors could be trained, to the exclusion of the children from the physical intimacy of their parents (significant when most huts comprise just a room with low partitions, if any, dividing the space for sleeping, cooking or working). It may also be a place where the tribal dances, songs and other forms of oral literature could be passed onto the next generation, and last but not the least, serve as a training ground for family life and social obligations in the future beyond the immediate singing, dancing and general rough-housing of adolescence. Although Elwin in one place has gone out – possibly in a fit of emotion - on a limb in describing the *ghotul* as a sort of a 'night-club', he observes with great sensitivity the organisation and principal activities of the *ghotul*. As the afternoon draws to a close, and the sun reclines towards the western horizon, the young *motiari* (or the adolescent Muria girls), possibly around eight or ten years of age come to sweep the premises and give it a fresh coating of cow-dung wash. The younger *chelik* (the adolescent boys) come back from grazing cattle or other chores, each bringing a few pieces of firewood, which is carefully stacked to one side by the side of the *ghotul* hut. By about seven, the older boys and girls come in, all washed and fresh, with their sleeping mats made of woven bamboo slats. The Sirdar or the Kotwar, the 'head prefect' so to speak, would check if all the things have been done properly and that all the boys and girls eligible to come to the *ghotul* were actually there. Some of the boys would try out a drum, a flute or a stringed instrument. Others would loll about, lying on the sleeping mats or chatting with friends, exchanging notes on the day just passed or planning something for the morrow. A few of the older *chelik* may have their legs rubbed and massaged by any of the younger *chelik* or motiari. A few may break into song while others pass time asking riddles. Elwin has especially mentioned the massaging of the *chelik's* legs by the chosen *motiari* and the combing of hair, which often led to a good deal of horse-play. As night deepens and the fire lit at the centre of the ghotul burns low, most of the *chelik* and *motiari* pair off on their respective sleeping mats and the murmur of voices trails off as they fall asleep in one another's arms. Elwin has not specifically reported any sexual intercourse as such; for, as he rued, he was expected to leave (possibly because he was a married person) just when the proceedings were beginning to get interesting! At the same time, Elwin has emphasised that by no means are the Muria licentious and the *motiari* are not easy to entice into sex. In fact, any attempt to force attention is strongly frowned upon. They have to be courted with gifts and songs, and even then the girl may well refuse within the framework of *ghotul* life and practices. All this certainly establishes the girl's right to have or not to have sex with a particular boy.

Despite what may appear to us city folks as considerable promiscuity, Elwin emphasised that by far the majority of the marriages were arranged by the parents of the boys and girls. There were also very few pre-marital pregnancies, in spite of the intimacies permitted. The *ghotul* also served to emphasise not physical beauty or prowess alone amongst those about to be married, but sincerity and team-work, lively behaviour, singing and dancing. Elwin has perceptively mentioned that the usual sexual selection of marriage partners as seen in most of the Western countries was largely overturned in the *ghotul* where the pairs were selected by the Sirdar or Kotwar assisted by the 'head girl', the Belosa or Dulosa. Personal preferences just were not allowed. This seemed to mitigate the jealousies and heart breaks experienced elsewhere. Pre-marital pregnancies were also few and far between and rates of separation or divorce after marriage were also very low. As with most such dormitories elsewhere in India or the world, the *ghotul* at one level kept alive the oral traditions of songs, stories, riddles and the dances. The boys maintained the drums, cymbals and other instruments required for singing and dancing. In learning to make small gifts for their *ghotul* partners, by way of a comb or a tobacco case or a bead necklace, the practice of crafts was maintained. The girls saw to it that the *ghotul* was always swept and cleaned. At another level, it readied the children to learn household duties through play as they swept the huts, made leaf-plates, gathered and stacked firewood. They learnt to work in a system of a hierarchy, with the Sirdar and the Belosa at the top, much like the village at large. At the same time, there was enough opportunity for horse-play and leg-pulling to make recollections of their days at the *ghotul* most pleasant for most of the older Muria. A strong sense of camaraderie, mutual support and cooperation for self-rule was inculcated, so much so that even village elders were not usually allowed to interfere with matters of *ghotul* practice and discipline. Lying and cheating became morally repugnant. Respect for tribal laws concerning marriage, divorce (the few occasions it occurred), pregnancy, birth and death became ingrained. Moreover, the *ghotul* provided a focus of ready man-power to make clearings for cultivation, herding the cows, helping in marriages and illnesses, and especially at the time of death and burial. Without the *chelik* and *motiari* making up the singing party, a wedding would be almost unthinkable.

Elwin discussed at length in *The Muria and Their Ghotul* (it was his D.Sc. dissertation for Oxford University) the factors likely to be contributing to the low level of pre-marital pregnancies in spite of the regular physical intimacies. He has importantly also distinguished between what may be commonly called the sexual impulse and the desire to 'settle down' and to have a family of one's own, and the role the *ghotul* played in this respect. This is not the place to go into all the details that are given in the book, and it should suffice to say that it is a 'tour de force' of a range and detail that is not commonly found in books on anthropology. Certainly, the deep concern and affection that Elwin had for the Muria come alive in its pages.

# 4

# Chasing a Dream: Abujhmarh

He who fights and runs away, lives to fight another day. Having an escape route is particularly important when going on a trip under uncertain conditions. Buying the return ticket to Calcutta at Raipur station was, therefore, a matter of necessity, especially after repeated harassment as the regular telegraphic messages for a return reservation never seemed to reach the booking office. This led to me being delayed in catching the bus from Raipur to Kondagaon. An enquiry at one counter, shoving and pushing one's way to another to buy the ticket, hands reaching over heads, and there was the reek of stale clothes, while the women sat around piles of baggage, herding their children carefully. A quick lunch at the bus stand did not help much and the departure time of the bus kept getting postponed. Finally, at about four o'clock, it decided to get on the move. Then there was the same excitement and expectation with the adrenaline rushing through the blood. There were new faces, but the same old jangling window glass, and the sharp tang of diesel and over-ripe fruit under the hot afternoon sun.

My co-passenger on the bus was an old hand at the game. He wore slippers made of old car tyres, a *dhoti* up to his knees, a dirty cotton waistcoat and an untidy bundle of clothes on his lap that he clung to. He was a Bengali travelling from the refugee camp of Mana to the village of Umarkot, both set up by the Dandakaranya Development Authority as a signal service in providing re-settlement to the hapless Bengali refugees fleeing East Pakistan following the partition of India in 1947. He had come over from what is now Bangladesh in 1957 after the initial influx of refugees had somewhat abated. He had wanted to stay on in Bangladesh and keep the life of his family ticking somehow. But that was not to be, and fearing for his life more than his livelihood, there was little he could have done except cross the border near Bongaon with his family one night. It was a story that had been repeated more than a million times. Out of public sight, it had also passed quickly from public memory. The loss of livelihood, the strain of keeping the family together, the wholly unfamiliar surroundings, the dust, the heat and the long queues with enamel cups and plates for food at the camp had not affected his spirit or his soft Khulna accent. Yes, he was growing some rice in and about Umarkot. He had been given about 3 bighas of land but rainfall was uncertain and life still difficult and unsettled. A vague memory of my own home in Bikrampur in East Pakistan – though we had left under less unhappy conditions - moved me to stand him dinner at Kanker and to give him some sweets for his widowed relative who refused to leave her seat in the bus; she knew what giving up one's place could mean. When we reached Kondagaon, it was precisely twelve o'clock at night. My new acquaintance elected to sleep in the bus, while I spread my '*durri*' on the cemented floor of the bus stand and laid down my burden. Two *adivasi* families were also settling there for the night, as any householder would, each with the small bundles of clothes, the babies in the centre, and pulling a sheet over the body to ward off the chill and the mosquitoes.

The night passed quickly, and after tea and a bit of breakfast (to which I was becoming increasingly familiar), I was on the bus to Narainpur. The bus halted every now and then to pick up passengers and disgorge some, and in the distance one could see little clumps of huts, sheltered under the trees, and hay-ricks, spindly legged, awkwardly standing in the fields. Along the horizon, smoke curled out of a newly charred forest. This is the time of the summer '*dhai*' or '*penda*' cultivation by the slash-and-burn method, which the Muria, and especially the Hill Maria used to grow crops on the hill-slopes and narrow valleys of the interior even in those days. This, like the adolescent dormitories, was a practice that the Muria and Maria shared with some of their brethren in India, such as the Garo, Naga and others in north-east India, and also with tribes in west Africa, New Guinea and the Amazon. The forest close to the road was more exposed to the hot breath of summer – it was May 1972 – and looked dry and weak.

Narainpur was all hustle and bustle because it was '*haat*' or the weekly *bazaar* day. In those days, Narainpur was for all practical purposes a one-street town. The road came curving in from the east from Kondagaon and making a wide sweep, turned north towards Antagarh. Spread out under the huge mango trees next to the large timber yard, long lines of shops made a moving fair. The Muria *chelik* were there in good strength, swaggering about, arms around one another's shoulders, throwing their heads back in laughter, their white teeth flashing, like so many children playing at being adults. Their dress was a tight white *dhoti* about the loins, as much for cover as for giving a firm support to the waist and hips for the long treks to and from the interior of the hills, an equally tight white turban with hair either tied in a knot or cut short at the nape of the neck, German silver bangles on the wrists, with beaded tassels fringing the *pagdees* (turbans), leaf cigarettes tucked in behind their ears or in the turban. The older men, feeling the weight of their liquor in the strong afternoon sun, growled softly amongst themselves. The Hill Maria looked their part as people of the hills, built more sturdily, with heavy hands, legs and feet, than the more lithe Muria, clad in nothing more than a loin-cloth. The upcountry traders from Raipur, Rajnandgaon or even farther away in Bhandara, went about their business with practised ease, in between heaps of ready made blouses, short cotton waist-coats, ribbons, small mirrors, bolts of cotton cloth, salt, potatoes, puffed rice, mustard seed, German silver jewellery, biding their time for a major deal. People milled around feeling the texture of some clothes or checking the weight of the salt they were buying, or filling a bottle carefully with kerosene, rather pre-occupied with the chores of life and thoughts of getting back home after another ten mile walk before the night came in. And in this play of light and shade and the steady hum of the bazaar, people hurried on their errands, draught buffaloes patiently chewed cud and Chhattisgharhi folk went about trying to look slick with narrow trousers and bush shirts. There was grace, surprise, expectation and joy in the *motiari* with their nut-brown rounded limbs, glistening with *mahua* oil, blue-black tail feathers of the red jungle cock fixed to the bead-fillet around their heads. Large eyes, frank questioning faces, soft quiet gestures, jingle of bangles, self-possessed and devastating. Some of them had colourful tassels or decorated combs in their hair, as they sauntered around in small groups, arms around one and another's shoulders, seeing and yet not seeing, hoping to catch the eye of some friend or beau. The older women, who seemed to wear the *sari* somewhat as an afterthought, haggled with the traders at the top of their voices, picking up and casting things away, eyeing the bright cut-piece clothes with vicarious pleasure.

My last-minute bag and haversack were put up in the inspection bungalow and after a cup of tea, I went in search of my good friend, M.R. Singh. He was delighted to see me and now that his family was with him, insisted that I should stay with him or at least share his meals. It was very difficult to refuse his hospitality and so I spent a couple of days in Narainpur travelling around and spending the evenings exchanging notes with him. Having spent some two or three years at Narainpur and having had to collect handicrafts – especially the '*dhokra*' - from the local people for his departmental work, Singh had a good deal of information on the nearby villages. As usual Syed Nawab Ali Khan would lend me a bicycle on which I could travel every morning and afternoon. The road from Kondagaon went past Narainpur and turned north towards Antagarh and Rajnandgaon, while a small branch crept west towards Sonpur. Towards the north, the road passed through a forest and as I cycled down, the trees seemed to draw closer to the sides and overhead. The ground was undulating, criss-crossed by shallow *nullahs*, boulder strewn and sandy. The air caught in the tangle of leaves and branches was silent and every now and then as the road coasted down across a shallow ravine, a cold breath seemed to hit one in the face. There was utter silence in those forests, cool shadows lightly dappled with sunlight. An occasional tribesman sauntered along with his axe hooked over one shoulder, baskets on the other shoulder, eating up miles in his tireless stride. Here and there, buffaloes and cows grazed in the undergrowth of the forest, with sudden rustles, frightening birds in the bushes and making me look over my shoulder. Not finding any village along the road, I returned tired in the late afternoon to Narainpur.

The next morning I took the road that ran south-westward towards Sonpur over a plateau, sunny and open but in places forbidding with dense stands of sal, nestling against the flank of some low hills. Groups of children and young people were tending to their herds and making the forest ring with their laughter as they chased one another around trees and bushes. A flat tyre found me with a six-mile trudge back to Narainpur, pushing the cycle with the sun beating down hard on my head and shoulders.

M.R. Singh warned me that the road to the south-east, towards Abujhmarh, was not very easy and in the evenings an occasional bear or two had been seen. In fact, a friend of his, cycling back from a nearby village, had been chased and knocked from a cycle which fortunately fell on him while the bear tried to claw him through the wheel-spokes and ultimately left him alone.

Acting on Singh's advice, I decided to take the bus on the same afternoon for Chhota Dongar, which lay at the threshold of Abujhmarh, the home of the Hill Maria. This is an area of about 1500 square miles, lying about thirty or forty kilometres to the south and south west of Narainpur, and in all accounts was a tough terrain, being a series of hills, ridges and spurs, deeply forested. Syed Nawab Ali Khan was as expansive as ever and immediately loaned me one of his better bicycles, which I loaded onto the roof of the bus. The bus waited for a long time near the main tank while passengers filled in and I struck up a conversation with the person sitting next to me. He introduced himself as Mangalram, a forest guard in the Chhota Dongar range. We talked of many things as the afternoon made way for evening and shadows obliterated the outlines of the hills and jungles. As the bus drew away from the town, further and further on through a ghat section, turning southwards towards the hills, we talked of the forests, the hills and the people. Mangalram said that he himself was an *adivasi* and had taken a Hindu name after his secondary education and employment in the forest department. He was articulate, forceful and what he said evidently had a lot of thought behind it. His view was that the Bastar *adivasi* was getting rapidly affected culturally due to intrusions from Orissa, south Madhya Pradesh and the Nagpur areas. Education, whatever poor quality there was, left the adolescents disoriented and alienated from tribal life and their roots in the countryside. They became peons, forest guards and *chaprasis* in petty government offices and learnt the way of the red tape, small-time petty power, and the incipient alcoholism born out of a growing inferiority complex and restlessness. The forests were changing from the verdant mixed varieties to plantations of teak and eucalyptus. No bird was heard to sing in these plantations, for there were no fruits and no berries. Increasingly, there were only row upon row, and acres and acres of plantations, which some day would yield timber to make tables and chairs, door posts and window panels, and raw materials for the paper factories. With the loss of bird song and the small animals, which were usually the targets of the ceremonial hunts of the earlier days, and told to stay away from forests, the *adivasi* felt confused and threatened. He was taught the three R's – reading, writing, arithmetic – in the primary schools scattered about, but neither his spirit nor his flesh drew any sustenance from it. Little was explained about adoption of improved agricultural patterns, practical day-to-day health and sanitation issues. At the same time, non-timber forest produce like pods of natural kosa silk, tamarind pods, tendu leaves, collection of resins and stick lac, bees' wax, etc. was gradually going out of the hands of the tribals and into those of city traders. Mangalram was getting excited as he spoke and even amidst the roar of the bus and people pressing down on all sides, I could sense how moved he was. Mangalram advised me to get down at his village, Dhaurai, and not to go to Chhota Dongar, where the rest house was a couple of kilometres away from the village. He said that he could arrange an accommodation for the night in the forest bungalow and some food. I agreed and when the bus stopped at Dhaurai, I had the bicycle brought down from the roof, while Mangalram sent somebody to open the rest-house which was just by the side of the road. It was a bright moonlit night and as I passed through the creaking gates of the bungalow into the garden, the flowering trees and shrubs seemed clothed in a phosphoric glow. The bungalow was large enough with three big rooms, of which I was given the middle one. After I had had a wash, I sat for a while on the open verandah taking in the moon-bathed landscape. I realised what a small pocket of civilisation I was in, with the flickering kerosene lamp by my side, the tiled roof overhead and the jug of water on the table in that vast expanse of forest, the clumps of ancient gnarled trees, and the streams rough-hewn between the hills and ridges. After a scratch dinner of parched rice and '*chhatu*', I spread out the *durri* on the bed, and fell asleep wondering what the next day would bring.

Mangalram was cleaning his teeth with a twig, and hawking and spitting outside his house, by the time I got ready to go out in the morning. The forest was a grey-green blanket cast over the hills and ridges all around. Far to the east, across the horizon already hazy with dust, the sun was trying to crawl up into the sky. There was a small tea stall nearby run by a Bengali - surprise of surprises - who had taken an *adivasi* for his wife and was not very communicative for understandable reasons about the rest of his family. Mangalram asked around to get me a companion to go the rest of the way to Chhota Dongar and then further on, but he was unsuccessful and he himself was not able to leave the post at that time. Ultimately, after a quick breakfast of *ghughni* and *chappatis*, I climbed onto my bicycle. Over and over again, as Mangalram bid me good-bye, he cautioned me to be careful in the forests beyond Dongar as wild animals such as bears and leopards were known to cross that area. Repeatedly, he cautioned me not to go into the jungle early in the morning or in the evening. Somehow, that short bus journey had brought us close.

The first six miles ride on the bicycle was easy. The road on this stretch was a fairly well beaten track, quite level. Here and there, the path dipped quickly as it ran over a riverbed, dry and sandy, waiting for the next monsoon. The forest was not so thick here and the only discomfort was the growing heat of the sun. After all, the month of May was not the best time to be out cycling during the day in central India. Chhota Dongar was then an up and coming village with four or five pucca houses, quite a few thatched huts, a tubewell and so on. Once past the cluster of houses and the rest house, which stood all by itself up on a hillock, the road curved to the right and led further to the south-west into the hills. From Narainpur looking southward, these hills had time and again appeared mysterious with their cloak of green-blue forests in a haze across the distance. Here, travelling through the main approach to the hills, they seemed much more brooding and silent, rough and perhaps not a little brutish. The bicycle moved on and now the road was getting progressively more difficult, rutted here and there with broken stones and chips gaping open to receive an unwary wheel. First, a teak plantation, silent as a mortuary, with line upon line of saplings with their leaves curled forlornly under the hot sun. Not a bird cheeped and no whine came from the ever-active grasshoppers and cicadas. The sun rose higher rubbing away all vestiges of cool shade from the path as it wound through the forest. Now, the road dipped down at a sharp angle and the bicycle raced down to the wide waters of a large stream rippling in the light. On the other side, raising its massive, craggy face stood a granite cliff fringed with thick forest. This was the Marian Gorge and the stream – I came to know later – was the Gudra, also called the Amdei, much beloved of the Muria and Maria. It was a quiet place with an uneasy sense of menace about it, protective of its own in its rough way, shielding with its fringe of forest and showing its unyielding granite face to the outsider. It was a place not for the city dweller and certainly not for a lonely traveller from far-away Calcutta. The soft lapping of the water sounded like the pulsating heart of a savage.

I had to put on my wide-brimmed floppy hat. The sun was beginning to burn. Ahead, the road heaved and rolled as it left the gorge and curled around the shoulder of the hill. Then, on more level ground, the path was broken and strewn with pebbles, with the leaves of the forest murmuring reassuringly in the breeze. To the right, the hill fell sharply to where the Gudra river had cut past the gorge, winking in the sunlight between the trees at least two hundred metres below the road. The cycle whirled on, dodging past the stony outcrops and broken ground, now rolling down a steep incline and now panting up the other side. My legs were beginning to ache. The water bottle had been filled the night before, but some mice had taken it into their heads to have a nibble at it and the water had leaked away drop by drop. It was still about half-full, but I thought it best to conserve it as much as possible. I stopped for a while and sat on a boulder, looking at the tree-tops with their fret-work of leaves against the sky. The eyes burned if one looked at the light for too long and quickly sought refuge in the dull olive grey foliage of the sal, saja, harra and karda trees.

The path continued, thrusting its way through the tangle of trees, while the sun grew warmer by the minute as it breathed heavily down the knotted tree trunks. The light that had provided pleasant warmth earlier in the morning was now burning my skin as it gushed through every open patch amongst the trees. Suddenly, a barking dear called from somewhere to the right in front of me. And again a second time, and then it burst into a hysteria of calls as it ran from some black-and-gold shadow. It had been so sudden that I braked to a stop trying to locate the direction and distance of the calls. All was quiet except a soft rustle as some leaves fell into the undergrowth by the side of the track. Then, I heard the grating rasp of a leopard as it moved somewhere down the hill, about forty or fifty yards away. There, perhaps, never has been a man who pedalled off so quickly. My one and only thought – as had been of that kakar – was to get out of that area as quickly as possible. There was no looking back into the forest for a glimpse of that spotted predator. It seemed so much more sensible to be on my way and reach the next village as quickly as possible.

The track wound in and out of light and shade, the cycle spokes glistened in the sun and my legs pumped on and on, but the distance did not seem to close. Down ravines and up again, once and then again, then blindly, as if in a daze, the sun seemed to draw out my breath and consciousness with every passing minute. Ever so often, I had to get off the cycle and push it up the gradients or guide it down the slope without falling over. My thigh and leg muscles had become swollen and taut with the constant effort and were beginning to throb with pain. The rucksack, which had been tied to the back of the cycle, kept swaying out and the water bottle tossed in its straps as the wheels went over a stone or broken ground. Overhead, the sun glowered with an out-pouring of yellowish-orange heat, scalding the trees and all the living creatures so that not even a dried leaf twirled down, not a cicada called and the path seemed to glow with light as noon approached. My eyelids had become dry and gritty, the nose tissues seemed to be seared and flaking off. I was even afraid to breathe deeply in fear of the shaft of burning-hot air thrusting into my lungs. Yet the sun, unmoved, lashed down relentlessly, the blinding light scorching everything that it touched upon. My eyes, tired of fighting that heat and light, wanted to close, my lungs could scarcely squeeze out energy and my legs just did not want to go on any more.

Tears came to my eyes. Where was I going, why was I going and how could I find any water and shelter in this endless wilderness? I had not seen a man since morning, nor heard a bird's call. The trees seemed to shrink and shrivel away from the path leaving no shade, absolutely no shade. No, this just could not go on. I threw down the bicycle and moved to the side of the track and lay down in the shade of a bolder. Beyond the penumbra of a hazy shade, the light blazed on and the heat seemed to turn upon itself with fury. Would I be able to get up? How long shall I have to breathe in this inferno? Only one orange and about four inches of water in the water bottle stood between a living person and the end of the road. I peeled the orange carefully, taking out each bit of fibre and bit into the soft flesh, the juice momentarily filling my mouth with its tangy refreshing flavour. I threw the pips into a hole at the foot of a tree nearby. Some day, if insects did not get to it first, after the first flush of the monsoons perhaps an orange tree will grow there and perhaps one day some weary and lost traveller will sit in its shade and find some comfort. Whether this was rational and reasonable did not seem to matter then; only it gave me hope and a desire to move on. It was painful even in the shade, with the heat singeing every exposed part of my body. The air seemed to dive into the lungs and tear it out tissue by tissue. I covered my face and mouth with a handkerchief, pulled the floppy hat lower and somehow made the cycle stand again. The rucksack kept slipping off and it could not have found a better time for this game. I had to push the cycle for about twenty to thirty feet before I could scramble onto the seat and then manage to keep those pedals moving and the front wheel out of the jaws of the jagged rocks on the track. Zigzagging across the path to maintain balance at that slow speed, thighs thrusting, falling out of the cycle, going up the ravine, I just could not seem to go on any more. The sun and the light seemed to say yes, the forest said yes, those sandy-banked ravines and every inch of shade said come and rest. How much longer would I have to go on like this? There were no mile-stones, no people, no villages, no water, no shelter; only the sun, the heat and the silent forest waiting. How far have I come and how much further shall I have to go? The questions echoed constantly and brought tears to a man at the end of his tether. Finally, upon making a turn along the track, across the spine of a ridge, about 200 yards away was Orchha - a village I had read of in some book, waited more than six years to visit and travelled more than a thousand miles to see.

It was just a village, with possibly eight hutments (this was in 1972 – it has grown subsequently) in a little clearing amidst large mango trees. That is all that registered as the cycle suddenly seemed to get a life of its own and without any urging, went faster down the slope. Little children stared and two or three men working in the shade of a hut gazed questioningly as I tumbled out near a mango tree at the centre of the clearing and lay gasping in its shade. *"Thanaguri, thanaguri"* was all that I could manage to croak out, asking, by reflex, for the usual resting place for travellers. I do not remember how long I lay there on the ground but it seemed that after some minutes someone was pulling at my arm and asking me to get up and move. Opening eyes took effort, and focussing took more time. Someone gestured to a house nearby, and with one last effort I managed to scramble up, leaving my faithful bicycle in the clearing; it would have to take care of itself. It was now a point of every man for himself, and the devil may take the hindmost. Inside the hut, the floor was unswept and gritty, but cool and away from that relentless sun, with the tiny door standing firm against the heat; a cool, cool, refuge.

I do not remember how long I lay on the floor, tossing and turning, as the heat wrestled through my skin and clothes to join its element outside. My mind was still hazy, hovering somewhere between unconsciousness and awareness, desperately trying to erase the memories of that sun, the blinding light and the searing heat. Now, just cool shade and peace. A hand shook me gently by the shoulder trying to reach the conscious mind. In broken Hindi he asked me not to lie down any as it would weaken me further. The words echoed through me and finding no answer, slipped away through the door. Again and again the hand shook me, forcing the comfortable torpor to let go of my mind till I finally groaned and sat up. He took my hand and led me shuffling across the courtyard to another hut. At first, the eye could not register anything in the darkness; then I could make out about four men playing cards on a metal table. Or they had been playing cards and were now examining me curiously, almost clinically.

"Who are you?"

"Why have you come here?"

"What do you want?"

"Where are you from?"

Staccato, the questions were spat out at me by impassive faces, demanding a reply. "Who are you? Why have you come here?" a face barked in the gloom. There was a chair nearby and I sat down. "Some water please, some water," I managed to croak out in Hindi. Who, why, what, how - they seemed so irrelevant then. Only water, cool shade and rest mattered. "Some water, please." "No water here!", the tone was matter of fact, closing the issue. There was a rasp of a chair and a stir somewhere to my left and a person who had been lying down on a bed nearby got up and instructed in Hindi "Get him some water". Then he went to the door, hawked and spat. Water came, then some more. I drank most of it, spilled some and washed my face. The questions came again, not noticing the interruption. I gave them the 'who' but the 'why' came back again and again. They were peons and clerks in some government departments posted there and it was incomprehensible to them that anything other than government business could bring out any person to that area. The questions persisted while I went through a dish of rice and dal, which the fifth person had given. I was almost too exhausted to eat and a griping in my stomach seemed to throw up whatever little I could put down. He again intervened and bade me lie down on a bed. One by one, the others left the room, while I stretched on a hot wooden bench, pressing a wet handkerchief as a swab to my nose and face, and sipping some more water with some salt stirred into it. Time and time again, the swab was changed and the sips of water continued till the sun having done its worst, sank, a trifle wearied, to the west and the cool shadows came flitting in from the forest.

The person who had given me water and food came back to the room and gave me a cup of tea. We sat chatting for a while as strength gradually came back to my mind and limbs. He was a clerk in the Tribal Welfare Department and we began a discussion on various aspects of government programmes in the tribal blocks, I haltingly in my broken Hindi, while he warmed to the subject speaking with feeling and conviction about his experiences. We took up Elwin's views on the development of the tribal areas, which had been put strongly, but to my mind not convincingly enough, and were controverted by the other. At one stage, he protested vehemently against Elwin's views on the *ghotul*, and it was then that he broke into Bengali. Yes, he was a Bengali, a victim of Partition, who had been on his way to Bombay to seek his fortune and had dropped off at Raipur and worked his way down here, fallen in love with the place, as Bengalis have an infuriating habit of doing. He had been cautious and had been trying to gauge me during the discussion and so had not disclosed his background, till he was satisfied. Now, he could practise his Bengali.

As evening came, Nangru, the general factotum for the few government employees posted at Orchha, went to the nearby stream that ran at the foot of the hillock and caught some fish in a narrow bamboo trap. I stayed back, the dehydration and exhaustion having taken their toll, loath to move, just sitting on a *charpoy* outside the hut, trying to take things in. The village stood on the shoulder of a wooded hill, while other hills circled it at a discreet distance with a wooded spur going off at a distance to the south. Huts, each with a rough and ready fencing, low, thatched, were scattered around and about for at least a hundred yards around. A few hay-ricks stood patiently under the shade of some trees. The cattle came lowing on their way back to the village, the bullocks with a harsh rasping sort of bellow that can almost be mistaken for the growl of a leopard. In the growing darkness, Nangru fetched some water, a part of which was used by Majumdar – for that was the name of the person in the Tribal Welfare Department - and the rest by me to bathe - yes, a bath for a person who was refused a glass of water to drink. As they say, it never rains, but it pours, look at it whichever way you like.

The moon was close to being full and it rose over the crest of the hills, creating its own peculiar, phosphorescent, under-sea world, with cool shadows wafted by the breeze rustling through the forest-clad hills, sibilant whispers in the huts, the brief flicker of a kerosene lamp, and the cattle stamping in the pen. The pain and exhaustion in every fibre of my body and the confusion and turmoil in my mind slowly dissolved in that gentle light of peace. Somebody brought a petromax lamp, for civilisation and the tedium born thereof must have its evening round of card games. Just outside the bamboo fence, the brightness of the moonlight made the peafowl think that dawn was at hand and they broke out with their clarinet calls echoing through the hills on the north, disturbing drongos and other smaller birds who briefly joined the chorus and drifted into silence and sleep.

Dinner was early and after the others left, Majumdar, a colleague of his and I lay down on our respective *charpoys* by the side of the hut, soaking in the moonglow. Majumdar sleepily asked what to do about a tiger that had taken to stealing cattle from a group of villages about five to six miles away. I gave a vague reply and was suddenly startled as a sambar hind called once and again a little further up on the hill in front. What striped or spotted shadow had caught its watchful eyes? Amongst the mango trees at the end of the village, a *'Bou-katha-kao'* bird (Indian Cuckoo) rang out its anxious plea to some unknown arch-browed, dancing-eyed beauty, appealing now in growing desperation – 'Speak, beloved, speak'. Only the moon riding high over the hill-crest smiled a deeper, knowing smile and the breeze, unable to contain itself, ruffled through the peepal tree behind the hut.

Somewhere, in the nearby huts of the Hill Maria, the drums began to throb, first desultorily, tentatively studying the resonance, trying to bring around a pattern. Gradually others joined and the drums began to beat to a rhythm, slow and thoughtful. My own heart and body seemed to resonate with the throb of the drums and I sat up on the *charpoy* to feel the sensation more intimately. Soon, there could be heard, piercing the deep throb of the drums, voices of young girls in falsetto, rising and falling to counter-point the beat of the drums. There was no hurry in the beat; it remained contemplative, playing with the heartbeats. It would be there tomorrow and the day after, so long as the hills were not levelled and the forests clothed those spurs and ridges, the streams mirrored the open skies, and the tang of wood smoke filled the evening air. The drums called out to share the quiet of the evening and the happiness of being together, the young voices sang of shared memories, desires and laughter. The five men carried on with their card game and I, unable to leave the comfort of my *charpoy*, remained in the shadow of the fence.

A good night's rest had driven the demons of exhaustion and uncertainty from my mind and I rose early and bright, what with the thud of a husking pole and the chirrup and chatter of the birds in the trees behind the hut. Even then, by the time I washed my face and had a breakfast of puffed rice, biscuits and tea, the sun was already beginning to make itself felt. Here and there, wisps of smoke rose from the hearths amidst the huts that were strewn higgledy-piggledy up by the side of the hill and round its shoulder. The forests all around were somewhat bare, having shed their leaves by the month of May. It seemed thick because the stems and trunks were densely packed, and not because of the foliage. Most of the trees were *mahua, simul, ber,* mango, jack-fruit, peepal, *champaka,* quite a few types of the *Terminalia* species, neem, and so on, with a sprinkling of the fish-tail palm (*Caryota urens*) and date palms (*Phoenix sylvestris*). People could be seen walking about in ones and twos, the men with a short *dhoti* tied tight around their waist and a rough turban on their head and the women in a short *sari,* reaching only to their knees, the heavy German-metal bangles and anklets occasionally glinting in the sun. Farther off, on the opposite slope of the hill could be seen the grey-black ashes and half-burnt stumps of trees of the slash-and-burn cultivation of the Maria. Majumdar took me to see the primary health centre that stood across the clearing. Within a short time, a few Hill Maria men came over, some with sores on their skin, some with eye infections – broad, placid faces – some astonishingly light-skinned in such a sun-baked land - robust shoulders and thighs, large calloused hands, broad, hardy feet capable of long hikes through the hills. They had come from the neighbouring huts and villages and it seemed that they were happy with the services of the PHC, where Majumdar's colleague, the compounder, ministered to them with his meagre and dwindling stock of pills and ointments. Majumdar then showed me around the village – not that there was much to see, for the huts were not in one compact group but were scattered up and down the hill in no organised pattern, each with its low-roofed thatched profile, the walls made of part wooden poles and part bamboo, a hay-rick and a small fenced-in compound. But as Majumdar explained, the Hill Maria, together with some other tribes in India, had practiced the slash-and-burn cultivation – known as 'penda' - on the slopes of these steep hills for generations, for the gradient was too much and the soil too poor for conventional cultivation. The population density was also very low – just about six or seven per square mile, as against thirty or thirty-five to the square mile in Narainpur *tehsil* as a whole. Wet rice cultivation was usually not possible because of the steep gradient (in most places being twenty to twenty-five degrees, and sometimes higher) and insufficient rains. Therefore, the Maria usually planted millets and pulses that could be grown even in those trying conditions, with just dibble sticks in some places, and in ploughed furrows where the lay of the land would permit this. These were commonly the *kosra* or *kutki* (*Panicum miliaceum*), or *mandia* (*Elusine coracana*), in-filled with runner beans such as the jata (*Dolicos lablab*) and some pulses such as *pukpul* and *piakmi* (*Phaseolus radiatus* and *Cajanus indicus*, respectively). The crop usually declined after two or three years and the Maria usually moved off to another part of the hills to make a clearing and begin the slash-and-burn cultivation all over again for another cycle of three to four years. Sometimes, the Maria left their village because of an outbreak of fever or depredations of tigers (one report has it that in 1963, there were about 150 cases of man-killing by tigers in Abujhmarh – by good fortune I came to hear of this only upon my return to Calcutta!). However, a few of the villages, such as Orchha, were more or less permanently settled due to the perennial availability of water (and therefore, some patches of rice cultivation), and access to *penda* slopes within about a kilometre radius of the village.

Majumdar led me along a winding path, past some fences and small vegetable patches to one of the huts of the Maria. A woman sat by the wall with her husking pole made of a thick log of wood tapering towards the top, pushing the grains into a small hole in the ground with one hand and picking up and letting down the pole with practiced ease. Her breasts were uncovered; her hair pulled back in a bun and pushed to one side of the neck, heavily tattooed face, arms and legs, which were stretched out on either side of the hole that held the grains. Around her neck were several strands of bead necklaces, and German silver large round ear-studs glistened in the light with every movement. She was dark, no doubt, but with a frankness of expression, directness in her glance, a straight bearing that gave a particular dignity and beauty. At our arrival, and on seeing an unfamiliar face, she pulled up a piece of cloth that lay at her waist to cover her breasts, in as much an unselfconscious gesture as any other Indian woman pulling the edge of her *sari* to cover her head on meeting a new person. Majumdar spoke a few words of Gondi, which were completely unintelligible to me, and she led us into the hut. We had to stoop to get in, for the entrance could not have been more than four feet high, and as the eyes adjusted to the darkness, we found the hearth on one side with the usual pots and pans familiar in any Indian home, with a couple of rough and ready wooden planks along the wall serving as shelves and in one corner a large woven bamboo basket for food-grains. Beyond that a small partition separated the sleeping quarters and a small fire burned there at the centre of the earthen floor, the feeble embers giving off the occasional wisp of smoke. In a corner hung an earthen pot, which Majumdar later told me held the ashes of one their parents. To one side, on a bamboo mat, a baby slept. The man of the house had left much earlier to tend the *penda* fields that lay about a kilometre away.

I spent the rest of the day exploring the village, trying to be helpful at the primary health centre, holding the pills and ointments that were routinely handed out to the Maria, or checking out the derelict hand-pump that had been inaugurated with great fan-fare the previous year – part of the target to provide drinking water in rural areas. One of the holding bolts had broken, and in any case, in summer, the water table fell too low for the pump to be able to function properly. I accompanied Nangru down to the narrow stream at the foot of the hill and helped him set the conical bamboo fish trap, and visited the 'Ghotul-ghar' or the adolescent dormitory, at the end of the village, where the children assembled every evening – although, according to Majumdar, they mostly went back to their respective homes later on in the night – and played their drums and sang the *ghotul* songs. The day passed quickly, so much so that I hardly noticed the scorching sun and furnace-like heat that had brought me to my knees the previous day. The evening, possibly like all evenings at Orchha, was spent with the local staff playing cards in the fore-court of the house, in the light of a flickering lantern. I stretched out on the *charpoy* and tried to collect myself from the thicket of sights and sounds of Abujhmarh, from passages in Elwin's and Grigson's books to the reality of the torrid heat, the desiccating dryness, the throb of drums and the lilting refrain of the songs, the pounding of the husking pillar, the tattooed arms and legs, the open smiling faces, and the haunting call of the '*bou-katha-kao*' bird.

The next day, almost at dawn, casting aside M.R. Singh's injunctions not to go out till the sun was up, I pedalled off back to Chhota Dongar and it seemed, in the relative cool of the morning, that it was hardly any distance. It was quite uneventful and I was in time to dump the cycle again on top of the bus, and it was well before lunch that I was back at M.R. Singh's house in Narainpur. The next day saw me back at Raipur, in time to catch the evening train back to Calcutta.

# 5

# In Elwin's foot-steps

The following year, in March, I was back in Bastar. A short rickshaw ride from Raipur railway station over narrow concrete-laid streets, slipping past and around faceless houses, buffaloes shouldering their burden without a sound, hawkers with their trays of oranges and other fruits, brought me to the bus stand. Diesel fumes hung in the air and one or two buses with engines idling made their windows jangle constantly. While a few were ready to move, some conductors bellowed at the top of their voices for passengers, much like magicians at a country fair.

At about ten o'clock our bus set off, passing the large tank at the edge of the town where children splashed and clothes were washed ceaselessly, and past the large sprawling refugee camp at Mana. Soon we were out in the countryside, ploughing through the gray brown countryside and stubble fields, till after crossing the Keskal *ghats* (with Metla *ghat* farther to the right), the bus snarled along the winding road as it stretched over the high plateau. The sun shone brightly on the deep green leaves of the long stretches of sal forest, mixed with the saja and asan, the harra, poroi, and fig trees. The earth was red and swollen in places, as if flushed with an inner fever.

The two previous journeys had made me an 'old hand' and I was soon on my way from Kondagaon to Narainpur to meet M.R. Singh. In the mornings, I would ride out on a cycle about ten to twelve miles, first down the Kondagaon road, and then turning off down the gravel-beaten path that rose sharply over the shoulder of a hillock. On the right stretched forested hills clad in the full foliage of the green sal and beyond that more hills rose tier upon tier, the dark green turning mauve in the distant heat-haze. Here and there, nestling amidst the hillocks in patches cleared from the jungle, were small villages of only about four to five huts. On the left, a river-bed with green sluggish water provided nourishment to the giants of the forest. This was the heart of the Muria country that Elwin had written of.

Having been through a Jesuit school myself, and then steeped in all the esotera of macro- and micro-economics, all this held out the natural attraction of any heresy. Crossing a causeway over a winding stream, I came upon a cluster of huts, typically sheltered by the side of the road in the shade of great tamarind trees. Leaving the cycle on the road, I went up the footpath that crept up the side of a hillock to one of the huts. Not a soul was in sight but somewhere behind one of the huts came the sound of a blacksmith's hammer. Two Muria were there, in the shade of a hay-stack, working pigs'-skin bellows, heating and shaping a number of wedge-shaped arrow heads. They stopped work and looked at the intruder, not with any animosity but with a mild curiosity, not particularly enquiring, not saying anything, and just looking, as one would look at something uninteresting and perhaps a little silly. I asked for some water to get a conversation going, but they did not seem to understand. I tilted my head back and gestured as if I was swallowing from a bottle and again asked them for some water. The elder of them then stood up and beckoned to me and took me down the hillside to a point where the stream lay coiled and motionless, glistening against a bed of sand. Well, there was water if you wanted it! I thanked him profusely and knowing that I had been unable to make a good impression, made off quickly. The road was wider here and went up hill and down dale slipping past forested hillocks with the occasional herd of cow browsing amongst the bushes. There were hardly any people working in the open fields, for obviously the harvest had been brought in some months earlier. It seemed that I was fated once more to leave Bastar without being in a Muria village and seeing the *ghotul* for myself, as Elwin had done some thirty years ago.

My first task back in Kondagaon was to contact one Mr. Bose to whom I had an introduction. He was in the Sub-Divisional Court when I arrived. I sat for some time in a curtained room adjoining his office during a hilarious cross-examination in a case involving a woman who had run away from her husband after being beaten repeatedly. The patient asking of questions and noting the replies in broken Hindi on both sides, and the

Prosenjit Das Gupta

theatrical thumbing of the table by the Government Prosecutor would have been instructive to any student of the rough and ready justice in the backwaters of India. Shortly afterwards, at lunch break, Bose came out to meet me and was quite overjoyed to see a person from Calcutta. At once, he took me to his residence, which was close by and we sat there discussing till late at night the many problems and prospects of the tribal areas. The next morning, he was leaving for Chitrakot for some official work and so he asked me to accompany him. I fell in with the idea and it was quite a different Chitrakot this time with the sadhus having disappeared and the government orderlies and cooks taking care of everything including the de rigeur chicken curry and rice for dinner. The night certainly did not seem so forbidding or the place so desolate. However, I had to sleep in an outhouse as some other officers had also arrived, and a more drafty and cold night had not been my fortune to endure so far. In the middle of night, the foot of the bed fell off and I went back to sleep inclined at an angle and wrapped up like a mummy. The morning saw us in Jagdalpur where Mr. Bose had some other official duties and I bade him farewell and took the late afternoon bus to Raipur.

When we were about ten miles from Kondagaon, the engine developed some trouble and we had to stop and wait for another following bus. It arrived soon enough and picked us up. But, just before entering Kondagaon one of the connecting pipes broke and the fuel dribbled out forcing us to walk the rest of the way to the bus stand. Thus, at five o'clock in the evening we were stranded at Kondagaon without any hope of leaving for another two or three hours. Ultimately, the fuel line, which was the source of trouble, was repaired and after a hasty dinner we set off at about eight-thirty at night. After driving some way, the driver said that he would stop for dinner for himself as he had been too busy getting the pipe repaired to have had it earlier. So, while the fifty odd passengers waited in the bus, he went to a nearby hamlet and ate his full; and apparently unknown to us, he had drunk his full too.

We set off once more, hoping this time to reach Raipur sometime early in the morning, but that was not to be. After driving for another ten or twelve miles, the driver suddenly braked and pulled partly over the edge of the road in the middle of a forest and promptly went off to sleep. Neither the conductor nor anyone of the fifty passengers crammed in the bus, with whimpering children and mothers dozing hunched up over their luggage, could bring the driver back from his sodden dreamland. A few of the bolder passengers got down from the bus. It was in the middle of a forested road. I had a small two-celled torch and the few of us gathered together some twigs and branches and had a fire going. The night was very cold and we stayed up for about four hours waiting for the driver to sleep off his liquor. At about four o'clock we gathered up enough courage to shake him awake and someone stuck a *bidi* in his mouth. The driver jumped up, cursing all and sundry. His language would have been a wonder to those unfamiliar with Chhattisgarhi swear-words but soon he quietened down and after drawing strongly on the *bidi*, he lit another one and started the bus. In hindsight, the driver possibly did the best thing by stopping the bus when he knew that he was becoming sleepy and that the Keskal *ghats* lay before us, thus avoiding a bad accident.

The bus arrived in Raipur at about nine o'clock in the morning, giving one just time enough for a wash, a lunch and some rest before the late afternoon train chugged off towards Calcutta. As the wheels rode clickety-click over the rail joints and the coach swayed lightly, I realised that my fever to see Bastar had somewhat abated, that the villages and the Muria existed, the sal forest, the hillocks and the winding roads were not something unreal, a fiction created by Elwin. A deeper interest had developed in the people, their handicrafts and their way of life. It would be just a matter of some months before I got back.

# 6

# Chhota Dongar

I was back in Bastar again the following year, 1973. I now knew about the short rickshaw ride from Raipur railway station through narrow twisting lanes, the grimy houses standing tired and slumped against one another, and the rough and tumble at the bus stand. Soon our bus set off, passing the large tank and the sprawling refugee camp at Mana. For some reason, the long rows of corrugated iron hutments and the barbed wire fencing along the perimeter reminded me strongly of a concentration camp. Dhamtari, Kanker, Keskal - the names mentioned in the pages of a book read some years ago, had now become real, with real people, *paan*- and tea-shops, bus-stands, fruit vendors – though Keskal was still more of a sleepy village in those days, bearing the promise of the rolling plateau and hills of Bastar. After crossing the Keskal *ghat*, it did seem that I was entering a new world, the world of the Muria and the '*ghotul*' and the songs and dances that I was yet to see. The sun slanted through the stretches of sal forest, with the occasional mixed patches of saja with its crinkled, crocodile skin bark, the aonla (or Indian gooseberry), harra (*Terminalia chebula*), and Bauhinia trees. The wheels of the bus threw up red dust from the fringes of the road that snaked in and out of the hillocks and forests. It was late afternoon by the time I reached Kondagaon.

With its sleepy tea-shops, the cycle-rickshaws waiting patiently under huge, spreading mango trees, and the bus-stand, which served as the pivot around which the town revolved, there was hardly anything to hold me back there. Fortunately, there was a bus leaving for Narainpur after an hour or so, but it was already filled with local people anxious to get back before nightfall. I managed somehow to scramble aboard and push my way in, rucksack and all, amidst mild protests of squashed toes and bruised elbows. In spite of the late afternoon light, it had grown quite dark inside the bus because of the press of people. With a jolt the bus finally started and the babble of voices grew subdued. It had grown quite hot with the considerable crowd inside the bus. A quarrel broke out about fares and the conductor roughly manhandled one of the *adivasi* women. I protested against his rough behaviour and another person, apparently also an *adivasi*, but perhaps somewhat literate, joined in the protest. The conductor finding that numbers were turning against him, retreated hastily. Even if the hurt done to the *adivasi* woman could not be remedied, the conductor had been taught a lesson. The other person and I exchanged a few words about the misbehaviour of the upcountry people with the *adivasis*. Then, he asked where I would be going and added that he too was going up to Narainpur.

In the general melee when the bus reached Narainpur, I missed the other person, but on reaching M.R. Singh's place, I found that he was already there. Singh introduced him as Jaidev Baghel, an up-and-coming '*dhokra*' craftsman, who occasionally came from Kondagaon (where he lived) to him with wares for sale. Singh said that he and his family, as well as some friends from the Forest Department had engaged a jeep to go to Chhota Dongar that evening to attend a '*marhai*' or a festival of the local Muria. This is a gathering of the clan-gods of the nearby villages, to propitiate them to look after the coming harvest and the well-being of the people. The festival brings together large numbers of the Muria, who sing and dance the whole night through before offering prayers to the gods. He was only too happy to take Jaidev and myself with them. So we started off in the dark, jam-packed in the vehicle, jolting over pot-holes on the road, the faint headlights barely picking out the trees by the side and the occasional bamboo fencing of a hut. I remembered the last occasion I had been to Chhota Dongar and the agonising journey into the interior upto Orchha, and compared it with the relative comfort of an evening ride in a jeep, albeit cramped. As we neared Dongar, streams of Muria on foot joined the road, and some of the chelik let off a blast from their horns or 'tori', a practice when travelling through a forest to warn off wild animals.

Young Muria cheliks playing drums at a 'ghotul'

We reached Chhota Dongar at around eight and put up at one of the houses there. The night was pitch dark ('*marhai*' is normally held in the course of a dark fortnight, usually between the months of February and April), unrelieved by even a single electric light. Overhead the star-spangled sky hung over the surrounding hillocks and forests and a babble of voices rose over the small field that was to serve for the '*marhai*' festivities. Telling '*Bhabiji*', M.R. Singh's wife, to keep my dinner so that I could have it whenever I came back at night, Jaidev and I set off, armed with a 3-celled torch and my camera. The Muria were already getting ready for the '*marhai*' dance by the flickering light of camp-fires. As we stood at the edge of the field, a large tableau rolled out before us – at the edge of the forest, the light of the small fires made the trees dance with the shifting flames, and lit up the small groups of *chelik*, here putting on their long petticoat-like dresses, or there tying tight the girdle of waist-bells, setting their turbans and the '*jhal*' or a spike of the tail feathers of the Racket-tailed drongo and male red jungle fowl. The *motiari* looked frequently at a hand-held mirror in the insufficient light – just as any other debutant would do - meticulously tying the bead bands across their forehead, setting and re-setting the German silver hairpins or the carved wooden combs in their hair. The older Muria could be seen cooking over the fires, or drinking with friends. It was one big picnic and '*tamasha*'.

Small groups of the *chelik*, who were all ready, tried out the first steps of the dances, shaking out the waist-bells, while the *motiari* in the falsetto voice that was to become familiar over the later years, sang snatches of songs that would accompany the dancing. Gradually more and more groups joined, the *chelik* fanning out into an ever-growing circle, shaking their waist-bells in an up-and-down movement, while the *motiari* formed groups of five or six inside the circle and at an angle to it, danced in step, singing, as the *chelik* gave the response with a roar of 'Relo, relo, rela ya'. More and more joined as people from other villages reached the '*marhai*' grounds, lighting the fires, pouring mahua liquor from the round-bellied dried-gourd '*tumba*', handing out leaf-plates of cooked rice and gruel, and the *chelik* and *motiari* quickly made ready with their waist-bells, the bead head-bands and necklaces, the pretty tassels, hair-pins and ran in to join the dancing groups. Some *chelik*, more impatient than the others, ran after their selected *motiari* to press their suit, and the latter made a big show of squealing and fending them off, hiding behind their friends, or running off in between the camp-fires, playing very, very hard to get. What liaisons were struck that moonless night away from the flickering fires would not be known, more so for outsiders like ourselves come to witness a strange festival; ever the by-standers and never participants.

I tried, in vain, to take some pictures by the light of a fire or of the torchlight, for in those days I did not have a flash-gun for the camera. Still, till about one o'clock in the night, when even many of the older Muria and the children had gone to sleep, curled up around their fires, I filled my eyes and ears with the dance of the *chelik* and *motiari*: the short quick steps, the tossing of the Racket-tailed drongo's tails, the flash of eyes raised in askance, the shimmer of firelight on the brass waist-bells, the gleam of white teeth bared in the joy of the dance and togetherness, the ebb and flow of the *relo* songs – a celebration of living and of the community that urban, modern India seems to have lost a good part of.

Jaidev and I – we seemed to have some natural affinity in spite of the distance in time (he being about eight years younger to me) and space (living more than a thousand kilometres apart) – rose early and went out in the half-light of dawn. By then the dancing had ceased and the Muria lay curled around the dying embers of the fires, and the forest that had been lost in the dark night, stood fringing close to the dancing field. A few of the local merchants who had come to sell their wares of aluminium utensils, salt, rice, cotton piece goods, ribbons, puffed rice, sweat-meats of jaggery and flour, were beginning to stir, some Muria mothers were washing the face of their babies – it was another day. As the morning wore on, the priests or the '*gaita*' began to assemble in front of the '*deoguri*' or the place of the gods for the religious part of the *marhai*, the gathering of the clan gods. These were personified in two black wooden logs tied with a cross-piece in the form of an H, representing Anga, and several gaily decorated poles, rather like the '*tazia*' flags taken out during the Moharrum festival but much smaller, for the sons and nephews of the god, Anga. The *gaita* wore colourful blouses, and tossing and shaking their heads went into a trance and began to mumble answers to questions put to them by other priests and seniors in the village. Not many people thronged about them, being more taken up by other mundane business of buying salt, or a blouse, or ribbons, savouring the hard sugar crusted sweet-meats, or disposing of their piles of *mahua* flower or tamarind pods or local silk cocoon to the traders.

In the middle of all this, turned up three Bison-horn Maria in full regalia with their head-gear of sweeping bison horns hung with tassels of cowries and playing the long drums hung over their shoulders, tuned in a foreboding bass – drim-drum, drim-drum. The local Muria was clearly not comfortable with their brethren from the south, across the Indravati river, and turned away or moved off while the visitors and traders from Kondagaon or Narainpur or farther away, and M.R. Singh, his family and ourselves gawked in awe at the Bison-horn dancers. They played the drums and danced slowly back and forth, and made sudden sweeps with the horn at some of the bystanders, much as a bison would do. They appeared somewhat taller and more robust than the Muria and the arching horns of the bison in their head-dress made them appear yet taller and quite formidable.

Jaidev and I went around the fair, which was now on in full swing, looking for things to buy as a memento. A couple of artisans were there with their wares of '*Dhokra*' or lost-wax decorative castings in the shape of small horses, elephants and lamps. A few feet behind them were traders selling puffed rice and standing there with a female companion was a young girl, possibly seventeen or eighteen, a Muria *motiari*, with wide brown eyes, a tawny skin drawn like soft velvet over her body. I stood stunned by that unexpected beauty amidst the swirling dust, with the mid-day sun pouring its heat down over that field. The hustle and bustle of the fair seemed stilled for a time as I gazed at her, unmindful of Jaidev, not noticing the beautifully woven beaded strings across her forehead and the thin brass chain round her throat, seeing only the wide-drawn, long-lashed eyes, with the gull-winged brows. The brows lifted into her forehead as if startled into flight, arching as does a gull's wings as it hangs momentarily in the air. Suddenly nothing else mattered – neither my job at Calcutta, nor my relatives and friends. Nothing else existed – neither M.R. Singh, nor Jaidev, nor the *gaita* at the *deoguri*, the people thronging the fair. Only the glowing, burning beauty of that tawny, burnished skin, the neat, rounded chin, the soft brown eyes, and the gull-winged brows remained in all the world.

She seemed to sense that someone was staring at her, for she looked up, straight into my eyes, and then visibly embarrassed, she pulled her companion by hand and walked swiftly into the thicket of canvas strung up on bamboo poles that made up most of the stalls. I made no attempt to follow, for in my heart of hearts I knew that she and I belonged to two different worlds in time, space, language and culture. I clung for solace to the words of Bibhutibhusan Bandopadhyay - '*Bonye-ra boney sundar, sishu-ra matri-crorey*' (as a child looks happiest in its mother's lap, so does a wild thing look best in the forest).

Jaidev was more concerned about having a bath and making arrangements for lunch, and so breaking through my reverie, he led off for about half a kilometre away to the banks of the Amdei. This was the gorge that I had crossed the previous year on my way to Orchha and the forbidding silence was now broken by about eight or ten people, including a couple of children, splashing about in the shallows of the stream and laughing and talking amongst themselves. A couple of Hill Maria women were there too, heavily tattooed, bared to the waist, strong-boned, washing clothes in the stream while we scrubbed ourselves close by on a boulder by the side of the river. The wet clothes dried on our body as we walked back to Chhota Dongar. M.R. Singh had by then left with his family and so Jaidev and I picked up our shoulder bags and walked down a couple of kilometres towards Dhaurai, where he had some relations and we could cadge some food. His cousin and family were happy to see us and not the least put off by the unexpected visitors. Their main concern was how to make some chicken curry for us, but that was easier said than done. The chicken had been let loose to roam around the homestead and they did not appear keen at all to disappear into a cooking pot. So, after running hither and thither trying to catch them and using the usual subterfuge of offering them rice and calling at them in an alluring tone, Jaidev's cousin hit upon the idea of getting at least one of them with a catapult. There then followed a great hunt, as the cousin stalked the chicken as they scratched around, bowed low with the catapult held ready in front of him. Even then, it took a couple of shots before he could get his eye in and winged one of the birds, which was then duly transferred to the pot. All this meant some delay in getting our lunch, but we would not have missed the 'great chicken hunt' for a month of Sundays.

Later that afternoon, Jaidev led me off to visit another relation of his, an elder uncle, who lived even farther in the interior, by the side of the Amdei as it makes a big circle and cuts across the Narainpur-Chhota Dongar road. Jaidev, as has been mentioned earlier, was of the Gharwa community who made their livelihood making the '*dhokra*' or lost-wax castings of decorative and votive figures. They were apparently originally from Hill Maria stock but had branched out into this vocation several generations ago. Although Jaidev's family had settled in Kondagaon for at least fifty or sixty years, they had several of their relations amongst the Muria and Maria of Chhota Dongar and Orchha. It was no wonder, therefore, that his uncle bade him and myself welcome. He would hear nothing of us going back to Chhota Dongar for the night. He insisted that we should spend the night at his place. His house was on a hillock overlooking the stream and he had a couple of plots by the side of the stream to grow rice and some vegetables. Conversation was somewhat difficult because Jaidev had mostly forgotten his Gondi and knew only Halbi, while his uncle was fluent in Gondi and knew little of Halbi. I, of course, knew neither. Uncle was fairly well-to-do and quite a personality. He arranged, without much ado, for a *tumba* of the salpi wine, made from the fermented sap of the fish-tail palm (*Caryota urens*) and a plate of chicken gizzard and liver for snacks to help the wine go down. The salpi looked like a light white gruel and had a sour, slightly bitter taste but was certainly refreshing. It soon persuaded Uncle, who apparently took to me, possibly mistaking my watch and camera as badges of the rich, to propose that I should marry one of his daughters and settle down in Kankerbera – for that was the name of the village – for a life of comfort and possible dissolution. He even took me to the edge of his court-yard and pointed out the plot that he would gift me following the marriage. It took a good bit of effort on the part of Jaidev, as my guardian in Bastar, to put him off by saying that he would have to consult his father in Kondagaon before finalising the marriage terms! The chicken curry and rice was excellent but no doubt the initial marinating of our innards with salpi had been most helpful. The next morning we were able to catch the bus to Narainpur without much ado.

I had a couple of days in hand before having to get back to Raipur and Calcutta. So Jaidev suggested that I should spend the time with his family in Kondagaon. As has been already mentioned, Kondagaon was then just a small town, with about twenty or twenty-five brick houses, about six or seven large shops, a primary school, a market place, and a timber yard. Jaidev's place was in Bheluapadar Para, four or five mud huts clustered under several large mango trees at the southeast end of the town. The two huts at the edge of the pathway were that of Jaidev's father, Shriman, and of his elder son, Sonaru, while those behind belonged to his elder sister, now widowed, and one of his uncles, and a couple of neighbours. Shriman was stooped over his work, fashioning intricate designs of bees' wax on a clay core which would become a small brass elephant in time, when I arrived. He and his wife bade me welcome to their small thatched hut and after washing our hands and feet, served lunch straightaway. Not much in terms of variety – being rice, dal and salt with some boiled vegetables – but the grace and sincerity with which this was served and our own hunger made light of the simple fare. This, in 1973, was my first introduction to everyday life in villages of rural India, after the Santhal villages of Birbhum I had occasionally visited in my childhood. It was also my introduction to a remarkable family of highly talented people, true artists in every way; honest, human, humane. My own friendship with Jaidev Baghel has not only stood the test of time over the last forty years and more, but has been deeply fulfilling in a fashion I could never have originally imagined.

# 7

# Days and nights in Bastar

The lost-wax process of casting brass figurines that I had seen at Jaidev's house lured me back. Of course, I equally wanted to meet with his family and know more about their craft and generally spend time in Bastar, and if possible to see more of the Muria. Small wonder then that I was back at Kondagaon in the spring of the following year. Shriman and his wife, Jaidev's mother, were as hospitable as ever. Whatever they had – and it was certainly not much in those days - they were prepared to share, and share gladly. Their meagre rations, the shelter of their one-and-half roomed mud hut, the bamboo matting of a bedspread, the low wooden 'piri' for a pillow, her experience in running an extended family, his knowledge of dhokra, the visualisations in bees' wax, the techniques of casting, were there for the asking.

The story goes amongst the Gharwa that many, many years ago, a huntsman was exhausted chasing after game. He cleared and set fire to the forest undergrowth near an ant-hill in order to catch some small game. As the fire roared, fanned by a light breeze, he was amazed to find metal oozing out of the holes in the ant-hill. After the fire had died out and the metal had cooled, he dug out the ant-hill to find that the metal had assumed the shape, size and form of the narrow tunnels threading through the ant-hill. Thus, the lost-wax process came to be discovered, where a small inner core of rough clay is smoothened over and patterned with a coating of bees' wax ornamentation. This is in turn covered with fine earth sieved from an ant-hill and then covered with further layers of clay and a mixture of clay and rice husk with a small funnel-like opening for molten brass or some such alloy to be poured in. This mass is dried in the sun and in course of time is heated in a simple furnace of sun-dried bricks, fired from below with firewood and boosted with a set of bellows. The wax slowly volatilises out, and in a swift gesture, almost like that of an experienced mid-wife cutting the umbilical cord of a new-born, the artisan turns over the figure so that the molten metal in the sealed funnel runs down by the force of gravity to occupy the same space and designs that had been made with bees' wax on the clay core. Once the outer clay covering cools, the artisan slowly chips at it to break the outer casing, and soon the gleaming brass figurine emerges from its swaddling cloth of hard-fired ant-hill earth. Such is the art and craft of 'dhokra'.

Over the next few days, I was led through the finer points of the 'pitchki' or the hand-fashioned extruder with which the Gharwa made bees wax threads of different thicknesses, the 'kutan' or the inner clay core of a dhokra piece, and the 'dhukna' or the set of leather bellows. The latter was quite ingenious. It was a large leather pouch, divided at the top into two halves and fastened to two wooden or bamboo rods. Just below this was the rectangular leather flap that functioned as a one-way valve, which closed when the top of the pouch was pushed down. The two rods had leather thongs attached to them, which were used to fasten the thumb to one and the other fingers to the other. Thus, when the hand was opened and the pouch pulled up, air entered through the leather flap and when the hand was closed and pushed down, closing the flap, the air was pushed out through a nozzle at the bottom of the pouch into the rough and ready furnace. The furnace was usually built under the shade of a tree by the side of the house.

Equally ingenious was the scale for measurement of the brass scrap that the Gharwa used to make the votive figurines. This was an ebony rod with a small pan hanging by three cords at one end and a brass blob weighing about 250 grams at the other, so that by moving the pan with the scrap brass to fixed positions marked out on the rod, the artisan could easily weigh upto about two or three kilograms. This weight was crucial as it had to be closely related to the quantum of bees' wax used, as otherwise the figure would come out incomplete (if too little brass was used) or the metal would burst out of the mould, if the weight was in excess of the required proportion.

Each day was almost invariably the same. We would be up at the break of dawn. Shriman and his wife would already be pottering about, setting up things for the day. After brushing our teeth with twigs – for that was the form – and drinking a full jar of water to work things up, as there was no practice then of morning tea, each would walk away as nonchalantly as possible with a tin of water about a hundred yards away into the bushes for that all-important 'movement of the bowels' that seems to turn most Indians slightly paranoid. Immediately thereafter, the menfolk would take out the work-pieces left half-finished the previous evening and set to work on them, adding and embellishing, or coating with the sieved ant-hill earth and a mixture of goat-dung and river clay to create an internally patterned mould. Some would polish the rough '*kutan*' so that it provided a smooth and even surface for the bees wax threads to be wound over it. These threads were quite stiff unless slightly warmed and the Gharwa made them pliant by keeping a small round brazier with a low charcoal fire by his side, and warming his hands and the wax thread by moving them periodically over this brazier. Long polished cones made of wood and the stiff spines of the porcupine were used to fashion the wax threads into circles, rounds, hatchings and ovals that usually formed the designs for the mould.

Shriman at work

In the meantime, Jaidev's mother and sister, Godhni, would be sweeping the hut and the courtyard and lighting the fire to begin cooking for the day. Shriman, who had usually disappeared by then, would appear trudging back after some time, bent over his staff with a *tumba* of salpi that he had cadged from some friend or neighbour. Sal leaves were produced in no time and were neatly folded into cups and the salpi was then sipped by one and all with much oohs and aahs. By mid-morning, the neighbours would drop in with the latest gossip and some of the men would march off to the lake nearby for a bath and to wash clothes. Lunch would be served by about eleven o'clock, Shriman would be served first as the head of the house, followed by Jaidev and his brother and myself, and almost invariably comprised a large bowl of rice, almost swimming in light dal, with some vegetables like beans or spinach or boiled tubers. It was simple, yes, but filling and perhaps even nourishing to an extent, but most of all it had the rich flavour of care and affection. I would give anything today to have Jaidev's mother back and serving us dal with her thin, wizened hands.

Then, it was back to work for another couple of hours. I used to watch fascinated as Shriman and Jaidev and some of their neighbours, such as Rupchand (one of Jaidev's brothers-in-law), almost magically fashioned the 'gehu dana' or the minute, tear-drop shaped item, the 'beni' made by joining two strands of wax threads twisted together like a plait of hair, and 'pikar-paan' made by joining three or four threads side-by-side and making small slices of the threads so joined. Their fingers moved swiftly and surely, almost feverishly: twirling, cutting, smoothening, fixing, shaping and out of a blob of clay and wax would emerge a horse or an elephant or the figure of a god, each with their own special decoration. Where their craft ended and art began I do not know till today; but theirs were certainly very beautiful pieces. Sometimes, more utilitarian items such as the popular hunting horn or the 'tori' (much used by the Muria in their visits from village to village), or a lamp, or an elegantly proportioned ladle for salpi would be made. In those days, the popular taste for dhokra had not yet developed and be it Shriman, doyen amongst the Gharwa of those days, or Jaidev (who was later to make much name for himself as an artist and sculptor) or Rupchand or any other, they would just collect them together for some fair or festival where many people would gather or go hawking them from door to door in some of the nearby villages.

Then would follow a couple of hours of siesta, when some would stretch out on the bamboo matting, some would just loll about doing chit-chat, the women-folk would stretch out their legs and sort through rice or dal, removing the stones, or would sew and repair clothes, till about three o'clock when most would resume their work once more, the men to their wax and clay, the women to cooking the evening meal. As evening fell, they would wind up their respective work, wash-up and sit out in the court-yard to chat and exchange notes on the day and talk briefly of the morrow - not much, just about (for they usually took each day as it came), and had neither the time nor the resources to do much planning for the future. One by one, the lanterns and the oil lamps would be lit, as electricity had not yet come to their neighbourhood, which was about a kilometer away from the main town. Occasionally, a bottle of *mahua* liquor would be caringly brought out and a couple of rounds would be done, accompanied by a leaf plate of *'chitti'* or the hot and tart chutney made of red-ants freshly brought down from a tree.

A part of the Barsur temple

Tales would be told of the old times, of the magical powers of Kulinder Singh Lal and Dhun Dhun Singh Kunwar, cousins of the old king, Bhairamdeo. Shriman recollected that his family had originated somewhere near Vizianagram but that he himself had been born near Bijapur (on the Jagdalpur-Bhopalpatnam road). His family moved due to the depredations of the local landlord to Paralkot, which lies considerably to the north of Bijapur and to the west of Narainpur, where they had been given land and the status of a '*malgujar*' or a minor landlord. For some reason now lost in time, they moved again to Hatlanar, close to Abujhmarh, and thence to Bakulvahi, in the neighbourhood of Narainpur. Shriman had apparently been sold to a *naib tehsildar* – a minor revenue official – and brought to Kondagaon where he had now settled. He added that there had been inter-marriages between the Gharwa and the Muria/ Maria and they formed a number of clans, such as Baghel, Netam (with the goat as totem), Sagar, Kashyap (tortoise), Nag (snake), Sori (tiger), Poyami (tortoise) and others. Their family deity was Gotaldeo, residing under a sacred 'saja', or *Terminalia tomentosa*, tree at Hatlanar.

At times, he would describe the various other deities such as Sandh Rao, mounted on a horse with a sword in hand, who would be patrolling the village boundaries; Burha Deo, the oldest amongst the gods, with a beard and paunch, and a staff and bowl in hand; Khanda Kankalin, the fearsome goddess with a protruding tongue pierced by a sword held in the right hand and a bowl in the left; the roving Telgin Mata, worshipped in the *ghats* and jungles, with a *trisul* in the right hand and a bowl in the left (there was a shrine to her along the Keskal *ghats*); Danteswari (the family goddess of the Bastar kings) who had seven sisters, (the eldest being Mawali Mata), depicted with a moon and star sign on the right hand and a *khapra* (or a burnt clay receptacle often used for carrying burning embers) on the left; Mata Dei, another sister, seen with a coconut in one hand and a khapra in the other, who was the goddess of small pox; the Banjarin Mata with peacock feather tassels in her hands; the Pardeshin Mata, a peripatetic deity often sheltering under '*pharsa*' shrubs and therefore also called the Pharsa Gondin; there was Pat Deo, with a broken left leg, staff in hand, usually residing in dilapidated huts and at cross-roads; Kotgurin Mata, four armed, bearing a *trisul, pharsa* or axe, sword and a *khapra*, who is said to ride on a tiger and protects the village from the predator; and the minor deities like Narsinghnath, Pilapat Deo, Purla Dei who are cousins of the great Anga and therefore represented like him by three logs – the central one carved with the face of a horse or a bull-held together with two cross-pieces, and decorated with silver crescents and stars and peacock feather tufts.

Dinner was usually served by seven-thirty or eight and then some of the men folk had a quiet smoke in the courtyard, while the women cleaned up or combed their hair in preparation of the night's rest. We were usually asleep by nine. There were no electric lights then in Bheluapadar and kerosene for lamps was expensive.

In between, I made a quick visit to Jagdalpur with Jaidev. He had to hand in some of his *dhokra* pieces to the exhibition-cum-sales office of the district industries department. There were several *dhokra* craftsmen working in Jagdalpur at that time, most notably Ganesh and Manik, but somehow I was not much taken in by their products. There was another small cooperative of local *dhokra* craftsmen in the town, and I fell in love with a figure of Ravana, ten-headed, twenty-armed, bold and defiant, confronting the arrows of Rama, Lakshman and Hanuman. This had been made by Gochi, one of the elder and renowned *dhokra* craftsmen of Bastar, in a novel, free-standing, chiaroscuro style with all the four figures being positioned on a small platform. I bought it for the princely sum of seventy-five rupees. This, however, left me without much funds when Jaidev led me to the house and collection of Shri Arun Chandra Guha. Arun-babu had been with the Dandakaranya Development Authority (set up by the Government of India to rehabilitate and re-train the Bengali, Hindu refugees from the erstwhile East Pakistan) as one of the instructors in woodcrafts. He was then living in a house belonging to the Sukma zamindari of south Bastar (in fact, I happened to meet one of the Sukma family on a later visit to Arun-babu and was pleasantly surprised to learn that he had been for a couple years at the Kala Bhavan, established by the poet Rabindranath Tagore at Santiniketan). Arun-babu, smoking his foul-smelling cheroots, would be ensconced amidst his collection of wooden, stone and *dhokra* crafts of Bastar, for he was more or less a clearing house for a number of the local craftsmen. He also had contacts with quite a few people and as I later found out, occasionally shipped some of the antique pieces to Indian collectors or to museums abroad. Possibly because of that his prices were a good deal more for the *dhokra* pieces than available from other sources and at times I literally had to plead with him to give an item I had taken a fancy to at a discounted price. Jaidev also introduced me to Shri Tushar Kanti Bose (younger brother of the late Swaraj Bose, who at one time had been a notable entrepreneur in West Bengal) who was then running a tabloid magazine, the '*Dandakaranya Samachar*', which was part in Hindi and part in English. He had correspondents in many places within Bastar and they used to file reports by phone or by letter, and these were supplemented by agency reports from the Press Trust of India. It was indeed remarkable how Tushar-babu almost single-handedly, as a reporter, editor, compositor (hand-composition, if you please) and printer, held up in those days, about forty years ago, a mirror to Bastar to the local administration and the rather limited reading public. We discussed on more than one occasion about the problems faced by the tribals from moneylenders and petty officials. I recalled to him the occasion at the Chhota Dongar *marhai* when a police constable had dragged a Muria by the hair around the field for failing to give him a light for his *bidi*, and when Jaidev had pointed out – at the same *marhai* – a cloth seller who had measured a piece of cloth first along the length and then along the breadth to give a false measure of length to a hapless Muria woman. We talked of the development of the Bailadila iron ore mines and its townships and the havoc this had caused amongst the Bison-horn Maria by taking away their land for a paltry compensation, besides the numerous cases where the innocent Maria woman had been inveigled into marrying a lorry driver or a crane operator and then abandoned. In spite of the frantic efforts by Dr. B.D. Sharma, the then Collector and Deputy Commissioner of the district, to rehabilitate these women, sometimes by compelling the offending 'husband' on a threat of prosecution and jail to take her back, the bulk of the problem persisted. There was rampant theft of the artifacts and sculptures – reportedly at times even by government officials – from the local temples and places of archeological interest, such as Barsur, Nagarnar and so on. All this was depressing and recalled for me the observations made by Dr. Elwin in his booklet, *Loss of Nerve*, where he had discussed – in fact following his visits to Bastar around 1941-42 – as to how the loss of their homestead – the most precious thing to a tribal (or for that matter, any human being) – and forests where they roamed and collected food, their confusion with the plethora of laws drawn up and enforced upon them by outsiders, the slow unraveling of their social and religious beliefs in contact with people who for some reason or the other tried to impose their own norms and practices on them, had led to a physical, mental and moral state of collapse amongst them. I felt complimented when Tushar-babu asked me to contribute an article; which I did and, this was duly published in a special issue of the '*Dandakaranya Samachar*' in 1975.

Jagdalpur in those days was for all practical purposes a one-street town, the road from Jeypore in the east more or less passing through the town towards Gidam and Bijapur to the west, although the through buses were diverted to a bypass running around the north of the town between the government circuit house and the district jail. A huge *'maidan'* lay to the south of the road – where some three years ago on my first trip, I had visited the *bazaar.* The house where Arun-babu stayed was to the east of the maidan, and the palace and the district collector's residence lay to the north of it. Jaidev and I made a round of the palace where the dowager queen, the wife of the late Pravin Chandra, his younger brother and wife then lived. The two-storied building stood facing east on a couple acres of compound, with a large portico in the center and wings at either end of the building. An empty aviary and a dried-up fountain stood forlorn in the front lawn. An antique silver-grey Rolls Royce with solid wheels and a long snake-like horn stood on sagging tyres in the portico. Jaidev pointed out the spots where rifle bullets had struck the walls of the building during the police action in 1964. Pravin Chandra, according to some, was somewhat of an eccentric, being a staunch devotee of the family deity, Danteswari, and with an equally firm belief in his divine right to rule. When pulled by the tribals on a chariot during Dussehra – reminiscent of the Lord Jagannatha of Puri – or when he rode or drove through the countryside, he would scatter gold coins amongst the people. Obviously, these actions were not in favour with the state government of Madhya Pradesh in a democratic India and it was almost inevitable that a clash of wills, as much as of beliefs, would result. This led to an uprising amongst the tribal villagers near Lohandiguda, on way to Chitrakot, and culminated in the death of Pravin Chandra in the police action that followed and the quelling of that brief rebellion. It was in this palace that the Bastar royalty such as Rudra Pratap and Prafulla Kumari had stayed and British administrators had come to advise, guide and perhaps occasionally to exert not-so-gentle persuasion. It was still a private residence but we could get one of the front rooms to be opened and were struck by the huge chandeliers, large oil paintings of some of the Bastar rajas, great antique sofas and tables, and the inevitable reek of genteel, tired descent from the past to the present.

The temple to the palace deity, Danteswari, lay close to left of the entrance to the compound. It was a small, simple one storied structure, with a porch in the front and the sanctum at the back. The Oriya priests who officiated opened the doors of the temple at our request. The doors had round medallion-like panels depicting the various avatars or manifestations of Lord Vishnu, as Varaha, Kurma, Vaman, Nrisingha and others. We could just about make out the image of the deity in the dim light, about 2 feet high in white glistening marble, riding a tiger, with mother-of-pearl eyes. Alongside was an image of the Lord Jagannatha, said to have been brought from Nowrangpur in Orissa. The floor – surprisingly – was set with glazed tiles with remarkable Japanese motifs like flying cranes, willows, in blue and white. Close by was the office of the regional anthropological officer and this housed a small collection of Bastar handicrafts such as bamboo fish traps, drums and other musical instruments, woven cloth, and so on, while in the courtyard lay the famous Ramarama funerary pillar. Elwin had written about such pillars being erected by the Bison-horn Maria to commemorate the passing away of some local chieftain. The pillar was huge, being about ten feet high, made of a single piece of teakwood log, and more than a foot thick along each of its four sides. This had four panels on each side, depicting an elephant, some Maria dancing with drums, Maria girls dancing with their 'tiru-dudi' staffs, two men carrying a pot of liquor, a tiger, a group of monkeys, while one had a couple of turtles and a fish. Elwin had referred to it, and that was more than thirty years before my visit. My estimate was that it had been made possibly thirty or forty years before Elwin's visit. Hopefully, this pillar, which is of significant historic and cultural value, is not languishing in the open, but has now been suitably housed in the state museum.

We took off the next day to visit Dantewada, which was a three hours' bus journey to the west, on way to Bijapur. This is close to the confluence of the Sankini river that runs ochre red from near the Bailadilla hills that lie to the southwest and the Dankini with emerald green waters from the east. The Danteswari temple lay on a large courtyard, facing east, and had no 'shikhara' common to most temples of Orissa and central India; instead it had a squat eaved roof over the sanctum. The forecourt had a grey granite image of Durga as Asta-bhuja, or eight-armed, and a pillar with a garuda capital. A covered corridor to the main temple had scattered images in black basalt of Ganesha and other deities, possibly excavated from nearby sites. Stylised lions, much like those guarding the entrance to the Konark temple near Puri, were placed near the entrance to the sanctum. The image of Danteswari was in black basalt, about three feet high, with mother-of pearls eyes, eight-armed, and flanked by other deities. The images were in the Andhra style with flattish noses, full lips, wide eyes and a heavy chin.

Thus, did the days and nights in Bastar pass, enabling me to see and savour the many sights and experiences, so far from everything that our city-bred lives had prepared us for.

# 8

# Of Bhaku and Ghotuls

One day, back in Kondagaon, Jaidev and I went to purchase some brass scrap – basically old and broken brass utensils which were still used extensively in rural India (often brought as dowry). Upon returning, I found an elderly man sitting in the veranda. He was very dark and lanky. His rough long hair was pulled back in a knot over the nape of his neck, his eyes were piercing black and his chin was covered by a salt and pepper stubble. Jaidev greeted him effusively as 'Bhaku-bhato' or brother-in-law, the husband of an elder cousin of his. Bhaku greeted me affably enough in broken Hindi (which very few of the Gharwa or Muria knew in those days) but I found that his bright, shrewd eyes never left my face. He was obviously sizing me up, a stranger, but a good friend of Jaidev. He apparently stayed alone in a small hut in the midst of a forest about two or three kilometers from Jaidev's home in Bheluapadar Para. Jaidev revealed that Bhaku was a famous 'siraha' or medicine-man and the ill came to him for treatment from all over the tehsil and even farther away. Once these introductions were over, Bhaku seemed to relax and became quite eager to share his experiences and memories, for apparently he had once been a trusted counsellor to Pravin Chandra Bhanj Deo, the last maharaja of Bastar. It was clear that Bhaku was unusually intelligent and had a good grasp of at least the major political movements in the country, although he himself read no paper, had no radio and lived at an arm's length from the rest of the town. Obviously he kept his eyes and ears open, but kept his counsel to himself. While he had some admiration for Indira Gandhi, the then Prime Minister of India, he was quite cynical of the way her younger son, Sanjay, was trying to climb the political ladder, and especially his single-minded drive for family planning, without really caring for health and other concerns of the rural poor. This he satirised in a song that he sang to me when we got to know each other better.

Bhaku Netam as 'gaita' or diviner

Bhaku invited us over to see the 'treatment' of a person who had come to consult him about a severe stomach pain. So, in the middle of the afternoon, the three of us - Bhaku, Jaidev and I – set off south west wards, across the main road to Raipur, past the timber depot, through a forest of sal, across a stream, for about a couple of kilometres till we reached his thatched hut with a palisade of dry branches in a small clearing in the forest. There was not another hut in sight, or in fact within a kilometre of his place. The 'patient', a Muria who had come from far-away Umarkote, was staying with him for a few days and was progressively getting better. Bhaku sat in front of him, naked except for a loin-cloth, his eyes hardly open, his long thin fingers drawing out a design on the mud floor of the hut with rice powder even as he whispered invocations to the gods of the skies, the forests, the stream and the earth. Between occasional sips of *mahua* liquor, Bhaku mumbled on, occasionally stroking the knees of the 'patient' or some time his belly. After sometime, he reached out and from under an upturned basket he brought out two small chickens, and with a swift motion cut their throats and dropped them at the two top corners of the rice-powder design. It was pathetic to see the two small chickens jerk and struggle as the blood slowly oozed out of their throats and crept through the design, staining the earthen floor. Bhaku kept on passing his hands over the chicken and the design and over the stomach of the 'patient', while with an averted head he murmured out the names of each of his gods to help rid the person of the stomach pain. After some time, Bhaku looked up from his ministrations and rubbed his eyes as if he had just woken up, and stroked his arms in a washing motion. The 'patient' looked distinctly relieved, whether through auto-suggestion or some sort of hypnosis.

That thatched hut nestling in the shadow of sal trees with jungle fowl, partridge, quail and the occasional barking deer for company, became a sort of pilgrimage for us. Sometimes when Bhaku was in the mood – this being usually a matter of wetting his throat with half a bottle of *mahua* liquor - he would don his chemise, blouse and headgear made of bright red and blue cloth, decorated with rows of cowries, and with a '*gupli*' or a bead-decorated basket under one arm and plumes of peacock tail feathers in the other, he would play-act his role as a '*gaita*' or priest at the pre-sowing divinations. He was our prime source for much information about Bastar and her people, some mythical, some real; for, there was hardly anyone else who knew as much of the local history and cultural traditions as he did. As Bhaku spoke, the Nasaldei Ghasni, who found the child-king of Bastar inside a gourd at a place called Kundakot, became as real as he was. He spoke of the extended family of gods and godlings, such as Hurre Mara, Kurum Tola, Bara Bhuya Anga near Bailadilla, Karia Wasi near Tulsi Dongri, Torma Pat-raja, Muria Mungraj at Paralkot, Visir-koddu at Kakwaras, Deoli Dokri at Antagarh, Koro Lingo, apparently the brother of Pat Jhari Patadunga, at Semurgaon, Khanda Dokra and his son, Wang Surya, at Dhanora, Bhumkarati at Phunder, Narsingnath, Bhaisadant Birmati and Ranbir Ransagar at Bara Dongar, Sonkuari Anga at Narainpur and other deities, who peopled the hills and streams and villages and sacred groves of Bastar. His animated face, and his arms flung wide to show how big and strong these gods were, his voice at times down to a conspiratorial whisper at the secrets he was sharing with us, was oral history at its best.

Then there were the times when primed by a bottle of *mahua*, Bhaku would go back to his youth in the *ghotul* in a village near Benur (on the Kondagaon-Narainpur road) and regale us with stories of his days there. As Elwin had noted, even the elderly amongst the Muria had fond memories of their days in the *ghotul*, much as we remember the friendship and escapades of our school days, forgetting the punishments for not having done our homework properly or the breaking of a favourite pen. There were never any salacious details of sexual encounters, just the pleasurable recounting of easy camaraderie of youth, the benevolent dictatorship of the Sirdar, the punishment by way of a fine for not bringing the specified quantity of firewood, the singing and dancing, possibly a shy holding of hands with the Malyaro or the Jalyaro, and at best a stolen caress. Bhaku would remember and slip into the *relo*-songs and other songs of the *ghotul*, about the Belosa who was running away to meet her lover and was pleading with the Bairagi Yogi, the boatman, to take her across the river, about the '*gaita*' or village priest who had sent his cattle to graze in the jungle and was anxiously asking the herdsman about them, Hulki songs, and some he seemed to have made up about the times of the last king, and of the later days of Sanjay Gandhi. He knew songs from other parts of Bastar such as of the Dhurwa and Dandami (or Bison-horn) Maria marriage songs. Then there were the chants – invocations to the great pantheon of gods and goddesses who mingled with the purling streams, the whispering woods, the high stone cliffs, and who joined the stars as they came out over the sal trees, along the edge of the thatched roof, as darkness drew closer with the passing hours. But by then, Bhaku would be getting sleepy and losing track of the words of the songs and it would be time for Jaidev and me to take leave and walk back to Kondagaon through the forest with just the stars and the rustle of sal leaves for company. We would usually walk back silently, each wrapped in his own thoughts, Jaidev's partly on the refreshed memories of the songs and chants of his forefathers and partly on the morrow – for he had to keep the family fire going – and mine going over Bhaku's songs again and again, now in Gondi, now in Halbi, now crooning, then in robust refrain, living out his fading memories, his failing powers as *siraha*, by the side of the murmuring sal forest that he obviously loved so much.

Massoo is Jaidev's cousin and we soon became good friends. He has a jolly and hospitable nature and lost no time in inviting me over to his village, Barkai. This was off the road for about four or five kilometres near Pharasgaon (where Dr. Elwin had also stayed on more than one occasion), on the main Jagdalpur-Raipur highway. So off went Jaidev and I one morning, but it was only in the afternoon that we could reach the village. Despite the late hour, Massoo's wife quickly made some rice and dal for us and we settled down to discuss the evening. Massoo suggested that we could go over to a nearby village, Kotelpara, to see some *ghotul* dances and hear some typical songs. Neither Massoo nor Jaidev had stayed at any time in a *ghotul*, although Shriman had done so in his childhood at Hatlanar. However, to them it was no novelty, just another feature of village life in Bastar, like growing *mandia* and *kosra*, like the village *deoguri* or resting place of the gods, or a bowl of salpi in the evening. So we trudged off for another two or three kilometres and reached just as evening fell. The village was well laid-out with fairly extensive rice-fields and the *ghotul* was under a huge spreading banyan tree. Soon the Sirdar, or the head-boy, of the *ghotul* turned up and readily agreed to arrange a singing session for us. The young boys and girls came in ones and twos, carrying their sleeping mats of woven bamboo - much as Elwin had described it – and were herded together into the small *ghotul-ghar* or the thatched hut where we were waiting. For the agreed 'fee' of a bottle of *mahua* liquor, they began with the girls playing small brass cymbals, and the boys beating on anything they could lay their hands on – a small oval drum, another shaped like an hour-glass, or just two pieces of sticks. The young voices, the boys often in falsetto, in happy chorus rendered the '*relo*' songs, which Elwin had found to be repetitive, that usually accompany their dances – as we had seen at Chhota Dongar earlier – enabling them to interact and intermingle, in question and response, first the boys, then the girls, then the boys again. I had by then acquired a portable cassette tape recorder, and upon playing back some of the songs I had recorded, the *motiari* burst into peals of laughter, poking teasing fingers at a friend who had fluffed a line or had strayed from the beat. The *mahua*, the throb of drums, the lilt of the songs, the press of the eager young bodies all around in the confines of the hut seemed to make time fly and it was soon time to go back to Barkai. With numerous '*johars*' – the salutation common in Bastar – ringing in our ears, our small group wend itself past the salpi trees with their crown of fringed and feathery leaves standing stark against the sky, the clumps of mango, tamarind and *mahua* casting dark mauve shadows in the waning moon light.

As agreed with the *ghotul* of Kotelpara, we were back the following morning and this time bearing gifts of *bidis* and ten rupees which found the girls and boys back in strength to give an account of their dances. Under that spreading banyan tree the *motiari* formed a chain of interwoven ebony, nut-brown and tawny satin, set off by the dark red short *saris* worn tight over the hips and breasts, with one arm round the waist of the girl on the left and the other over the shoulder of the one on the right, with short steps back and forth, swaying a little to the left, now stepping to the right while the boys, with a variety of drums, played in a loose group in front of them. Some dances were slow and languid, with long phrases in the songs, while others, like the 'hulki', were fast paced, where the girls moved swiftly to one side or the other, progressively forming a tight circle, while the boys played drums with great energy and moved with quick steps, lifting the drums to breast or shoulder height in the excitement, eyes flashing, and tassels in the turban flying across their faces. There was a fine Muria boy, playing a large drum – locally called the '*dudra*', hollowed out entirely from a single piece of wood – who led most of the dances. In this melee, it was difficult to make proper recording of the drums and the songs, and to run my tiny 8 mm camera, knowing all time that there would be no re-takes – if all this could not go on record on the film or the tape, it would have to take its chance with just my memory.

It was also at Masoo's that I met Garib Ram, who regaled us with Pandwani songs and ballads to Alla-Udal, the legendary heroes of the Gonds; although more of the north and east, than of Bastar proper. His vigorous playing of the drum, the excited and flushed face as he sang of the great deeds of the Pandavas and of Alla-Udal, was a performance that I shall long remember. There also occurred a strange incident while we were at Massoo's. One evening, at the request of Massoo, I played some of the chants of Bhaku Bhato that I had recorded on my cassette tape recorder some days earlier. One of Massoo's neighbours, who was also listening, suddenly stood up awkwardly and started swaying and stamping about, waving his arms about as if in a trance. Massoo signaled me to shut off the cassette player, and he and Jaidev held the man as he collapsed on the floor and washed his face and arms with water, till he opened his eyes and shook his head as if to clear away some thoughts that had come upon him suddenly. We did not speak of this later; it was best forgotten.

On one of my visits to Bastar, Jaidev and I decided to visit Bara Dongar, connected with some of the history of the district. Hiralal has mentioned two inscriptions from Dongar, one of 1779 AD relating to a visit by Duryodeva and another of 1871 about the *'pattabhiseka'* of Bhairamdeva. Bhaku had also referred to some of the well-known deities still worshipped there. Bara Dongar is accessible by a walk of about ten kilometres northwards from a point about midway on the Kondagaon-Narainpur road. Close by were the villages like Remawand and Nayanar visited by Elwin in the 1940s. The *kutcha* road meandered through patches of sal forest, across *nullahs*, dry in the late spring, and the occasional fields of rice harvested some months earlier. The village was fairly large, with some fifteen or twenty huts, two or three *pucca* houses, and some shops. Just to the north and east of the village was a rocky hillock on which stood the temple of Narsingnath. It was a simple shed-like structure, apparently put up as an after-thought to protect the god from the weather, who had so long roamed free amidst the sal forests, the streams, the large boulders dotting the land, amidst the mango and tamarind trees of the village. There were two stone tablets near the door of the temple in Telugu script, and very curious statues of a couple of cadaverous creatures, part dog, part lion, which guarded the entrance to the temple. There were also curious offerings of burnt clay images of horses, bulls and even of elephants, made by the devoted to the god, who was hardly about a foot high, quite dwarfed by a huge burnt clay elephant that kept it company. On the other side of the village was a large lake, locally called Dudh-sagar, and the ruins of a temple with sculptured lintels and pillars, strewn about its banks, while some devotee had rescued a few of the sculpted images and placed them in the cool shade at the foot of a banyan tree. It was a cool and peaceful scene, and Jaidev and I enjoyed having a swim and a bath in the lake with the sun and the gentle breeze drying off the clothes on our backs.

After cadging some food from one of the households there, who apparently knew Jaidev's family, the two of us started off again in the late afternoon back along a path that ran to the east and south from Bara Dongar, so that we could come out at the Kondagaon-Narainpur road at another point. There was fairly good jungle in this area, mostly sal, but with a scattering of the *Terminalia* species, the occasional Fish-tail palm, mahua, and tendu (*Diospyros melanoxylon*). The land was more undulating and broken in this area and we must have walked for about four or five kilometres when we came upon a small village. We had hardly put our bags down, when the elder brother of the village *patel*, or headman, arrived in a reasonably sozzled state, to bid us welcome. It was a most affectionate – almost fawning – welcome, for he ran his hands over our face and shoulders and arms, taking particular interest in my watch and water-bottle. Delighted with our gifts of a packet of '*bidis*' and a couple of lozenges, he proceeded to regale us with stories of his hunting of deer, partridge, rabbit and wild boar, play-acting the stalk and the shooting off of the arrow. At one point, he fetched his bow, which was almost as tall as he was, and the typical Muria arrows with long blades and deeply forked ends, and gave us some demonstrations of his prowess, which really did not add up to much. But thanks to his intervention, we were able to secure a chicken for our dinner, and shifted to the *ghotul-ghar* on the northwestern part of the village of about ten or twelve huts, scattered about along the edge of the jungle.

Typical evening scene in a 'ghotul'

The *ghotul* comprised two open-sided sheds and one covered shed, with bamboo matting for walls. As the sun dropped to the west, and we started plucking the chicken to make an early dinner – for we were quite tired with our walk that day – two or three young boys of about ten or eleven years of age turned up with the prescribed bundles of fire-wood for the *ghotul*, taking time off from splitting some of the larger pieces to smoke a couple of our '*bidis*'. After another half hour or so, at about six, two girls aged about fourteen to sixteen years arrived to sweep and clean the open sheds – in one of which we were putting up – and the closed hut, and throw out the leaves, wood ash and half-burnt fire-wood. While our dinner was bubbling on an open fire by the side of the open shed, some more boys and girls came in – more precisely, according to my notes taken in the flickering light of the fire, six boys of about sixteen to eighteen years of age, five younger boys of ten to fourteen years, five girls of about fifteen or sixteen years – it being always difficult to tell the age of women – and four younger girls of about ten to twelve years, possibly just entering puberty, came in and sat chatting by the fire. By the time we had finished our dinner at about eight, Jaidev had managed, with his poor Gondi but persuasive Halbi and gifts of lozenges for the girls and '*bidi*' for the boys, to get them to put up a song and dance performance for us. This was going fairly well for about an hour, with the motiari singing '*relo*' and humourous songs to the accompaniment of '*chitkuli*' or small brass cymbals, which I was taping, when one of the older 'bucks' swaggered in, looking somewhat charged up, and tried to drag away one of the girls of about fifteen. She strongly resisted and some of the *ghotul* members also remonstrated with him, as much for using force as breaking up their singing. He let go of her hand and sat in sullen silence for some time at the back of the *ghotul*. Then, he again came up behind one of the older girls who was watching but not singing. He whispered something into her ear, and she answered laughing. He cupped his hands from behind over her breasts and she shyly drew a length of cloth over her bosom, leaned back against him and started to massage his legs stretched out alongside her. The singing and the playing of the cymbals and the thrumming of the drums carried on, with occasional peals of laughter if any one went off-beat or missed a line of the song. The flames of the fire crept lower and lower and one by one the *chelik* and the *motiari* stretched themselves out around the fire, while Jaidev and I, each with our thoughts and memories, left the *ghotul* and went to sleep by ourselves in our open-sided hut.

The morning broke fresh and cool, and by that time the *chelik* and *motiari* had largely dispersed to their respective families to catch up on the day's work in the fields and herding cows, while we gathered up our bags and left – Jaidev to Kondagaon and I on my way back to Calcutta.

# 9

# Into the Heart of Abujhmarh

It was late spring in 1975 and I had been going to Bastar each year since 1970. Yet the fever had not quite abated, despite the fact that I had seen and experienced much that had largely borne out the observations made years ago by Elwin. The hills of Abujhmarh, to which I had had a rude introduction in 1971, still beckoned, their very obscurity and inaccessibility sending out a siren call that at times became too much to bear. Jaidev was of little help because he too had not ventured into the interior of Abujhmarh and was not a little apprehensive of the unknown. Still, I plotted and planned.

The Narainpur *Marhai* has been always special for me. It was one of the largest of the gatherings of the Muria and Maria and had considerable religious significance amongst the tribals, with elaborate '*jatra*', or '*deo khel*' or 'dance of the gods', led by Anga himself. All I knew was that it would normally take place within the 'dark fortnight' in late spring, around end March or early April when the waning moon would make it easier for the gods to visit their subjects and would also hide from public gaze the caresses and assignations of the *chelik* and *motiari*. There was no advertisement, no tourist brochures - only word of mouth, and that took a long time in reaching Calcutta from Kondagaon or Narainpur. Still, I privately made my own calculations and in April 1975, duly arrived at Jaidev's place in Kondagaon, and was delighted to learn that the Narainpur *Marhai* would be taking place within another couple of days.

'Gaita' in 'deo khel'

As mentioned earlier, a *marhai* is a village fair combined with a *bazaar*, with a good amount of serious religious events and plain inter-village social interaction thrown in for good measure. It seemed to me somewhat strange that Elwin should have mentioned the marhai as a social event for the Muria only in passing. While he has described in great detail about marriage, birth and death, there are just about two mentions of the *marhai* in *The Muria and their Ghotul*. Yet any visitor to Kondagaon and the Narainpur regions of Bastar – even upto Antagarh in the north – would be struck by the importance that the local people and the tribals attach to these festivities, from both social and religious points of view. Edward Jay, however, writing in *A Village in Middle India*, about his studies at Orchha in the early 1960s, does give it a greater prominence. The last time I had witnessed such an event, though on a relatively local and small scale, was in Chhota Dongar about two years previously. Due to lack of prior information or plain bad calculations, I had missed out in the intervening years. So I was determined to make good, and the next morning saw Jaidev and myself taking the bus to Narainpur. We put up with Halal, the son-in-law to Bubu, Jaidev's aunt on his father's side. He lived in a two-room hut, on the western side of the village – for Narainpur in those days was still essentially that, with one inspection bungalow, about ten or twelve *pucca* houses for the government staff (including that of M.R. Singh, who incidentally had been transferred in the mean time), one or two tea shops, one eating house (run by the Kerala brothers), and possibly twenty or twenty-five huts inhabited by the local tribals.

The 'gaita' at Narainpur "marhai"

Already the petty traders from Raipur, Rajnandgaon and even farther afield in Bhandara had turned up, much as I had seen in Jagdalpur on my first visit, with short stocky bullocks used for ploughing or pulling carts, trays of hard, crusty sweetmeats, heaps of puffed rice; ready-made shirts and blouses, rough, grey blankets, *saris*, trinkets and cheap ornaments, and articles of daily use such as torch batteries, rice, salt and kerosene oil. There were swings, roundabouts and itinerant photo-shops being quickly set up, to tickle the natural curiosity of the *adivasi* and relieve the tedium of day in and day out of plain hard slog. The Muria had been trickling in since morning, threading through the hillocks and ravines, wading across streams, trudging through sal and mixed forests from the north, south, east and west, to the Narainpur *marhai*, to see, to be seen, to buy and sell, to be renewed. The men carried great baskets of '*kosra*', '*kutki*', '*kodon*' (the grain commonly grown and eaten in those parts), tamarind pods, dried *mahua*, swinging at either end of bamboo poles on their shoulders. The women too came in good numbers, carrying babies on their hips, with large baskets of '*kosa*' or pods of the wild silkworm, the *tendu* fruit, dried tamarind, and so on. The young *chelik* and *motiari* broke into a run as they neared the fair grounds, laughing and jostling amongst themselves, some carrying the inevitable *tumba* of salpi or *mahua* liquor, others baskets of food and clothing for the couple of days they would camp at Narainpur for the *marhai*. The old and the young, the firm of limb and the cripple, shriveled crones and lissome maidens all flocked to this one festival they all called their own.

By the late afternoon, the Muria and Maria families had gathered in clusters under the spreading mango trees at the south-east end of the village, next to the timber yard. Each family and each village group sat together, with the baskets heaped on top of one and another, while some of the menfolk had taken their loads elsewhere and had spread out the '*kosra*' and the tamarind pods and the '*kosa*' in great heaps on pieces of cloth spread out on the ground. There was a great to-do and a general air of expectation of the festivities the following day.

As evening came, fires flickered in between the mango trees, as each family warmed up the food or cooked afresh for an early dinner. Jaidev and I moved in between this ebb and flow of people, taking in the glances, the murmur of voices, the sudden gleam of teeth, the acrid wood-smoke, and the hiss of boiling pots. Here and there, the *chelik* and *motiari* were making ready for the dances later in the night, the boys tying on the pleated petticoat-like dresses, unslinging the axes – the '*pharsa*', shaped like the forked tail of a drongo – readying their turbans, tucking in the '*jhal*', or the tassels of black tail feathers of cocks and the racket-tailed drongo in the folds of the turban, tightening once more the cord of the waist bells. The *motiari* had washed themselves, lightly rubbed on *mahua* oil, put on fresh *saris*, combed back their hair into a tight knot at the back of the head fixed with German silver hair pins with their small round bells, checking the bead necklaces round their throat and the beaded bands across their forehead. By about nine, some of the *chelik* groups were gathering in the clearing next to the fair grounds, trying on their *relo* songs, rendered with that peculiar quaver and a combination of bass and falsetto pitches. Some shook out the waist bells – up and down, not from side to side – while groups of the *motiari* stood close by, one pushing the other to join the dance first.

Sipping 'salpi' in Abujhmarh

By the time we had made a round of the fair grounds and it was getting to be past ten o'clock or so, the dancers seemed to have made up their minds, and group joined group, village to village, until a great circle of some four hundred *chelik* and possibly some two hundred or so *motiari* had gathered on the dance grounds. Then began that great chorus of voices, the falsetto of the *motiari* mingling with bass of the boys, the huge clamour of the waist bells, and the thud of dancing feet, as the *chelik* formed an outer circle while the *motiari* danced inside in small rows of six to seven, arms and shoulders intertwined. On and on, watched by bystanders like ourselves from nearby villages, by their elder uncles and aunts or the younger siblings, the boys and girls swirled around, now in fast step, now with a slow-paced lilt, singing of the days they had lived and shared in the folds of those hills, of the heart-aches and teasing touch of a hand, of the flowers that danced on the boughs and the streams that had breached their banks. For, they were young, and alive; alive with hope, expectation and desire. Standing close by, one could see their flushed faces, the robust steps of the dance, smell the sweat, the dust, the wood-smoke, hear the sharp intake of breath as they broke into a fresh line of a song and feel on our faces and hearts the thrust of young voices soaring skywards. From a little afar, only the roar of the waist bells remained, rising and falling like surf on a rocky beach.

How long we were watching this scene I do not know, when I suddenly saw her – the girl with the gull-winged brows – her large eyes wide-open in recognition and defiance. She was dancing with her friends – now stepping to the front, now swirling sideways, locked arms over shoulder, as the young bucks swept around with their waist bells jangling in high crescendo. Suddenly everything seemed to cease – the high-pitched *relo* faded, the waist bells sank into silence, the circle of *chelik* seemed to have disappeared. I saw only her eyes, the long lashes stilled in surprise, the brows arching to her temples. I somehow broke through this reverie

Climbing the 'salpi' tree

and as boldly as I could, though with a beating heart and shaking hand, managed to get within a few feet and take a couple of pictures. Then in the next instance, with the click of the camera shutter, the circle came to life and swung around, the *motiari* locked arms to shoulder, and the girl with the gull-winged brows was drawn into the vortex of that dance, the dance of things forgotten and remembered, of youth, of dark star-lit skies, of mango and *mahua* flowers. I was left only with two pictures and teasing memories of the girl with the gull-winged brows.

With all this, I woke up late and grumpy the next morning. But a hot cup of tea followed by a draught of salpi that Halal had somehow procured put new heart into me and I readily joined Jaidev for a round of the fair grounds. There was a buzz of activity all around, mothers were cooking the main morning meal over their fires, or distributing the food in leaf-plates to the members of their family. The *chelik* were packing away their '*jhal*', '*pharsa*', the pleated skirts and the waist bells in the wicker baskets. The *motiari* were up and about, hands held close with their *ghotul* friends, doing a bit of 'window shopping', running their hands over a sari or blouse that had taken their fancy, or eyeing a juicy sweatmeat, or ogling at the villagers crowding around the swings and round-abouts. Here and there, behind the cover of mango trees, whispered bantering and pleasantries were exchanged with boyfriends, and assignations were agreed. The *motiari* were quite striking in their white *saris* with narrow blue or green or red borders, drawn over one shoulder and reaching only to the knees, the bead bands stretched across their foreheads, the bead and red pom-pom tassels hanging from their hair-clips, swinging invitingly. The Hill Maria were also there, though not in much numbers, the men with a strange quiet in their eyes and hands, talking softly amongst themselves, the women, many heavily tattooed on the face and arms, with only a small *sari* tied like a skirt around their waists but with thick necklaces of beads, feeding children the remnants of the '*pej*' or the gruel of *kosra* and *kodon*. They seemed so elemental, and perhaps really were at one with the elements of the sun, the earth, the rain and wind that were their every-day neighbours.

A Hill Maria girl with typical facial tatoo

The religious part of the *marhai* began at about ten o'clock, when the sun was quite up, with an assembly of the Muria with one large red flag and a white flag on long poles, with a decorated brass '*kalas*' or pot on top of each, under a large mango tree close to the center of Ghasia-para, close to which Halal lived. He informed me that the red banner represented the deity, Banjarin-mata, while the white one was Bhoram-deo. One of the villagers came forward to break several coconuts in front of two bamboo trays, one containing the cowrie-decorated red dress of the '*gaita*', or priest, and other with a small brass image, two horse-hair whisks, an ebony stick and a plate of rice. The brass image was apparently of Garhia-deo, the brother of Bhoram-deo. Sometime afterwards, possibly shortly before lunch, four of the *gaita* sat in a row under the mango tree, and started trembling, muttering and slapping their thighs and seemed to have gone into a trance within about five or seven minutes, one tossing about, another rolling on the ground, with yet another falling rigid in a sort of fit. Some of the elders then began to put questions to them to know which deity had come upon them, and they managed to mumble some names, which the elders either themselves identified or in one or two cases referred to other villagers for verification. The principal deity appeared to have come simultaneously upon two of the *gaita* and a mild argument ensued as to which one of them was authentic. However, this was amicably resolved with the deity declaring that she was one and the same for both the priests. Then one of the senior priests, with half of his head shaven and a thick lock falling over his nape, dressed in a red blouse and skirt, decorated with cowries, had his ankles bound lightly with iron chains. This group of priests then proceeded to the *deoguri*, or the village temple, further east nearer the main road, where five '*anga*' – each made of three logs, with the central one carved with the face of a horse, and held together with two cross pieces – were waiting with their respective carriers. There were ten *gaita* tossing and leaping about, some in pairs, while a local band played the *muhuri* (a sort of '*sehnai*') and kettle drums at fever pitch. With the arrival of the '*lats*' or the red and white flagged poles, the *anga* took on a life of their own, making their human bearers run about this way and that, and throwing them around as if they were mere dolls, animated only with the life force of the *anga*. Then led by the chief priest, a tall, old Muria with grizzled whiskers, holding a large knife upright in front of him, this procession of *anga*, the *lats*, the other *gaita*, and the hangers-on proceeded to the fair grounds and circled from east to west and then in the reverse directions, while the local tribals threw handfuls of puffed rice over them. They were then joined by other deities, such as Sonkuwar, Lalkuwar, and others all in the form of '*lats*' and by a tall pole with a rectangular woven frame of bamboo decorated with local white flowers, and these proceeded to a part of the fair grounds where a high swing had been erected, the bed of the swing being fixed with nails pointing upwards. The *gaita* took turns to sit on this 'swing of nails' and elders from the villages of the locality asked them of the rains, future of the crops that year, the health of the people and so on. After this round of questions and answers, the *gaita* seemed to wake from the trance and rubbed and brushed themselves, before all the *lat*, the *gaita* and others returned to the *deoguri* and dispersed from there.

By this time, the Muria and Maria were wending their way back to their respective villages, some having come as far as twenty-five to thirty kilometres away, and it would take them the better part of the afternoon and a good part of the night to reach their hearth and home. I was left with a few pictures, some recorded minutes of taping of the *relo* and other songs, some footage of the *gaita* and the 'dance' of the *anga* in the 8 mm camera and a whole lot of memories.

Our group in Abujhmarh (Jaidev at extreme right)

Jaidev and I had been planning for sometime a trip to the 'marh' as the Abujhmarh region is commonly called in Bastar. Neither Jaidev nor I knew anything of the pathways or the language there, and so we managed to put together a motley group comprising Sonaru (Jaidev's elder brother), Dhiru, an uncle of his, to provide the horse-power in carrying things into the interior, and Murha, a 'ganda' or of the cow-herd caste, who knew Gondi, and had travelled in those areas from time to time. So, a couple of mornings after the *marhai* had ended, the five of us set off for the *marh*, with Murha, Sonaru and Dhiru taking turns to carry the shoulder poles laden with bundles of used jute bagging for bedding, bags of rice, dal, potato, onions, chili, salt, cooking oil, *tumba* of water, etc., for there was no surety we would get any food or water once we were in the *marh*.

We had no definite plans and no set destination and so just took a path that led more or less southwards over scattered rice-fields and patches of forest, past the villages of Bakulvai, Kotvai, Jamri and a couple of others. Soon we had left the din and bustle of Narainpur far behind, with only the crunch of our footsteps, the swish of the baskets brushing past shrubs and tall grass and the sound of our own breathing in our ears. By about noon, we were at the foot of an escarpment, and it was quite a climb traversing it diagonally, cutting across its face, with just a faint footpath to lead us on. This turned more to the southeast, through more dense forests, mainly of sal with bits of mixed forests, and also quite large patches of tall grasslands. Hoof-marks of sambar and barking deer crossed the path here and there, but we saw no animals on the way. By about four o'clock, having walked steadily for about seven hours (or about twenty or twenty-two kilometres) under a relatively mild sun - for it was still spring - we came to an isolated village of just four or five huts. All around were dense mixed forests, with only four or five of acres of cultivation, now shorn of their crop. The *patel*, or headman, was ill, and said that several other families had also left the hamlet, Kotenar, due to persistent fevers. There was no ghotul-room, and the *patel* being unwilling to part with any part of the sambar haunch that was drying in his room, we set about to make camp as best as we could before night came on, for neither the patel or ourselves had any kerosene lamps. For shelter, we had a large spreading simul tree, which had mostly shed its leaves and was coming into bud, and our fire was built in the shelter of three large rocks. While the rice, dal and potato were boiling, Murha managed to persuade the mother of the patel to sing a few ghotul songs for us. She was quite aged, white-haired with dark, much creased skin, but still her eyes lit up as she started to croon in a low voice the songs of her long-lost childhood. Her shriveled body swayed to and fro with the remembered rhythms and the knobbly, veined hands beat weakly together as if in salute to those near-forgotten days. The songs were in Gondi, and Murha who was the only one of us familiar with the language, tried as best as he could to translate the songs for us – the songs of spring, of youth, of flowers, of friendship, of long-forgotten desires. Under that dark, star-lit night the flames cornered between the three rocks, seemed to leap up to give accompaniment to her songs, while the forest remained silent, listening intently. The night passed uneventfully, except for the alarm call of a sambar quite some distance away.

The next morning, after tea and a snack of puffed rice, we continued our journey, now to the southwest, into the depths of the Marh, over a high hill, which required a stiff climb, and I remember our knees occasionally touching our chins as we struggled up the slope. Here, there were extensive dry deciduous mixed forests, the more obvious tree species being the salai (Boswellia serrata), saja (Terminalia tomemtosa), harra (Terminalia chebula), tamarind, tendu, kachnar (Bauhinia species, including the 'siari' or 'elephant ear' creeper, Bauhinia vahlii), karda (Cleistanthus collinus) and the like. Black tongues of rock protruded from beneath the baked earth, and here and there larger grey boulders showed their hardy shoulders. There were no villages, no human beings, hardly any pathways. Murha and Sonaru guided us more by a sense of direction and rough bearings from the sun, than any definite idea as to which village we were heading for. Beyond the hill we had to cross a stream, already dried up by spring-time, and it was just as well because we discovered that a couple of our tumbas of water were leaking. Sonaru and Murha proceeded to dig the sandy bottom of the stream, and lo and behold, within about a couple of feet we had clear water seeping out. We refreshed ourselves and filled up the tumbas and continued our trek, this time along a long spur, and then through extensive grasslands almost shoulder-high. We chanced upon a female sambar that had been resting under the shade of a harra tree, and we were as much startled by her sudden alarm call and clattering away, as she had been at her rest being disturbed by some dirty humans.

By late afternoon, we came to a clearing and we found a couple of the Hill Maria trussing up a barking deer that they had shot with their bow and arrow. This was done in quite an ingenious way, for, as Murha translated, they made a habit of urinating each day next to a particular rock by the forest track, which on drying left traces of minerals which the barking deer was greatly fond of and came to lick. They had been doing so at this point for the last week or so, and now had their supply of meat for the village. Once they were assured that we were not forest staff – for I was wearing a khaki shirt and trousers - they gladly led us to their village, Kalmanar. As we approached the village, there appeared to be some turmoil going on as it seemed that a band of about four or five Bison-horn Maria had appeared from across the Indravati and were in the process of taking away two or three bullocks from the village without due payment. Our party was happy to be led to the other side of the village away from this unwanted trouble; for the Bison-horn Maria are known to be irascible and may not hesitate to let fly with their axe if the mood so takes them. The villagers kept complaining in a loud voice and grumbling as we watched, from the shelter of our hut, the Bison-horn Maria pushing and goading the bullocks away. By evening, things had settled down somewhat; but our enquiries revealed that the village did not have a functioning ghotul – as Elwin had reported, the Hill Maria do not have a proper ghotul system and the few boys and girls available just meet to share their experiences of the day and sing a few songs and then return to their parents' hut for the night. Still it was good to visit a typical Hill Maria village with their slash-and-burn fields scattered along the slopes of the neighbouring hills. In spite of the obvious hardships and the constant struggle with the forces of nature in such a forbidding terrain, the Maria seemed quite healthy and cheerful. The menfolk appreciated our gifts of 'bidis' while a few of the women were happy to pop into their mouth the lozenges we had taken with us. Both men and women had good physique, and surprisingly, several of them had light brown eyes and even lighter skin than one finds amongst the Muria. The women wore nothing to cover their breasts and I felt awkward in front of their naiveté and lack of self-consciousness in photographing them; though I did take one or two for the record. I had to face further embarrassment the next morning when a number of villagers came to petition, because they thought that with my khaki shirt and trousers and a retinue of four, I was a government officer. A couple wanted a well, another sought protection from the depredations of the Bison-horn Maria, while two others wanted medical assistance, one for an eye infection and the other from a large boil. From my meager stock of medicines, I gave them whatever was necessary, while with the assistance of Murha and Dhiru, I managed to wriggle out of any firm commitment for the well and protection from the Bison-horn Maria. I did not want to raise any expectations – only to cause disappointment later; for it was clear that, at least in the area that we had traveled through, no government staff, let alone any officer, had

Cooking a 'scratch meal' in Abujhmarh (Jaidev, third from left)

visited in recent months, and if at all, in the last couple of years. While they were quite capable of looking after themselves, it seemed that at least the benefits of modern medicine, sanitation and facility of drinking water should not be denied to them, just because they preferred to live away from the public gaze, amidst their beloved forests and hills with their tendu, tamarind, chhind, salpi, siari and ready supply of ants' nests for the tart snacks to go with the 'salpi' juice.

We were off again early next morning – for even in early April, the sun does get quite hot by late morning and one can work up a good deal of sweat walking up and down the ridges and spurs. This time we turned northwards – roughly in the direction of Narainpur, for we had taken provisions for only three or four days. This time, we seemed to be descending from a plateau, for the land seemed to level off and the hills receded behind somewhat, although the ground was still quite rocky, broken with the occasional chhind (Phoenix sylvestris) trees and considerable stretches of grassland. There were quite thick forests all around and patches of sal appeared with some almost pure stands of karda (Cleistanthus collinus) with their delicate light green leaves standing out against the blackish, gnarled branches. Conserving our meagre rations of water and snacking only on puffed rice and dalmot, we reached a fairly large village, Jharavai, just as the sun was dipping towards the west. We were cordially received by the patel and led to the fairly large ghotul, to put down our load and to rest for the night.

The ghotul was quite large, in an equally large compound enclosed by a palisade of rough-hewn logs – as indeed were most of the houses in the marh. Also, as with most huts in the marh and even in the Muria areas, the ghotul was made of plaited bamboo walls with a thatched roof. Two large drums were placed on a plank of wood at one end, together with a couple of stacks of leaf-plates. While we were putting our rations together for dinner, four or five young chelik appeared shouldering several pieces of firewood, which were neatly stacked just outside the ghotul. As we had seen elsewhere, a few of the smaller girls then appeared to sweep the ghotul clean of the previous night's wood ash and leaf-plates. They were not the least put off by finding strangers occupying their hut, for other than myself, the others looked much like themselves, and dressed in the same short dhoti and sleeveless banian, and spoke in the common Halbi tongue with a smattering of Gondi. By about seven o'clock, by which time we had cooked and had our small dinner, the older boys and girls came in a swarm, laughing and jostling amongst themselves. After them came, tap-taping his bamboo staff in front of him, the Sirdar or head of the ghotul, a well-built lad of about seventeen or eighteen, blind in both eyes.

They seemed quite happy to have us in their midst, thanks, of course, in part to the 'bidis' and lozenges doing the rounds, and in part to Murha's ability to speak their language and thus build an almost immediate rapport. The girls and boys had settled around the ghotul, and on our invitation, proceeded to give a rendering of their repertory of ghotul songs, other dance songs and the sad dirge-like 'nahuni' song, which is sung when the Muria install a stone megalith in the memory of a dear departed. I could only note the songs phonetically and it was much later – in 1994, when I visited Bastar for the last time – that I was able to have the songs translated with the assistance of Belsai Wadde of Markabera (for the Gondi was quite beyond Jaidev). One song started with the words 'Gurva yul, dada-le' (or something phonetically similar), which was a Hill Maria marriage song, with the children asking one and another, 'Why isn't Manjaro-bai (girl as glamorous as a peacock) in our midst today — do you know brother, why? Pandaro, the deity, is counting the dancers with their waist-bells. Where is Manjaro-bai, brother?' Another was a Hulki song with a rapid beat, beginning with the words 'Barat kara na… leki juri lele', where the boys and girls sing alternate lines – 'Here, girls take these bangles./Why should we take these cheap bangles?/They will look nice on your arms./Here, girls, take the 'pairi' ankle-bells./Why will we wear thin ankle-bells?/For they will look elegant on your feet.' There was then a slow-paced 'nahuni' song beginning with the words 'tayong matey', which could be rendered as 'the stilts are dancing for you/the small bells are tinkling/the small bird 'gunju' is sitting and singing for you/rows of crops are growing (as they did in your time)/and the 'simul' has come into flower'. Another 'nahuni' song went 'Yama kango dore ja' or 'boughs of the mango and the imli tree are dancing as children hang from them/if you wanted otherwise, you would planted the (short, tuber) onion/let us tie a fresh garland of flowers and be united as friends/we will make fresh tassels of peacock feathers'. There was also the song for the 'marhai' dance, 'Lal baji pungarey, pungarey intor' ('Why are the red flowers dancing, brother?/They are putting on a show for you./Why is the siari trembling, brother?/They want to be a necklace for you/and now even the white flowers are like a bead necklace around your neck.'). For the next two hours or so, I sat enthralled with their verve, sense of tune and rhythm, the obvious feeling with which they rendered the songs, and was amazed at the spirit and personality of the blind Sirdar, who conducted the entire evening with the élan of an experienced Master of Ceremonies. It was he who suggested the songs and caught the words if there was any faltering; it was he who beat the rhythm with the ingenious rattle made of bamboo slats tied tightly together. I taped the songs with the anxiety and feverishness of knowing that in all likelihood I would never ever get another opportunity to record authentic Muria ghotul and other songs. All this while, the boys and girls did not for a moment indicate by word or gesture that we were interlopers or were disturbing them and certainly there were no overt sexual moves except that one or two of the elder boys sat with their arms around their girlfriends, or cupped their hands over a girl's breast and whispered sweet nothings into their ears. By about ten or ten-thirty at night, the singing drew to a close, and we went to one end of the rectangular shaped ghotul and fell asleep, while the chelik and motiari crowded around a couple of fires at the other end and curled up to sleep. Sonaru later reported that in the middle of the night he had gone out to relieve himself and found a pair of chelik and motiari coupling by the side of the hut. All this appeared more spontaneous and on the spur of the moment, as may happen with any adolescent anywhere, rather than under any formalised system of permissive sexual intercourse.

Early next morning we bade a fond farewell to the Sirdar and his fine team at the Jharavai ghotul. By this time, I had developed sore feet from an ill-fitting boot and it was in considerable pain that I managed to do the rest of the trek – fortunately with very little hill climbing, except to get around the shoulder of the Karelghati, supported by Dhiru on one side and Murha on the other. Overall, it was a small price to pay and we managed to reach Narainpur around three o'clock in the afternoon.

Even now, after more than forty years, whenever I play the tapes, the throaty voice of the Sirdar, with the 'tarrak…tarrak' beat of his bamboo rattle, the chorus of young voices, the laughter and the friendly teasing of the songs reach out effortlessly over a thousand kilometres. In my mind's eye, I seem to see the fires at the Narainpur Marhai flickering into life around the mango trees, while the chelik try out the waist bells, and the motiari straighten out the bead bands one last time, and the surge of young voices singing their favourite songs seems to wash all over me. The easy familiarity of embrace between the chelik and motiari in the sanctum of the ghotul appeared to me as a part of youth, longing and being happy in each other's closeness that can, and does, happen anywhere, any time. All my senses – eyes, ears, tongue, touch and smell – were now sated with the impressions and experiences of nearly a decade of travelling among the Muria in Bastar, and my mind now seemed to seek to know more about the person who set me off in the first place on this endless journey.

# 10

# The Ganjam Interlude

Parlakimindi is not a name familiar to most Indians, and it was not to me, till I realised that it formed the beach-head for any foray into the hills of the Eastern Ghats. This in turn formed the better part of Ganjam in Orissa, the land of the Saora. The Eastern Ghats with their great mass of hills and forests stretch a long way, rising as some low hillocks at the border of West Bengal and south Bihar (now Jharkhand), then with a short break, into the hills of Saranda in south Singbhum, then onto Keonjhar and the Simlipal massif, and further southwest wards through Kalahandi, Koraput, Ganjam and the hills of East Godavari

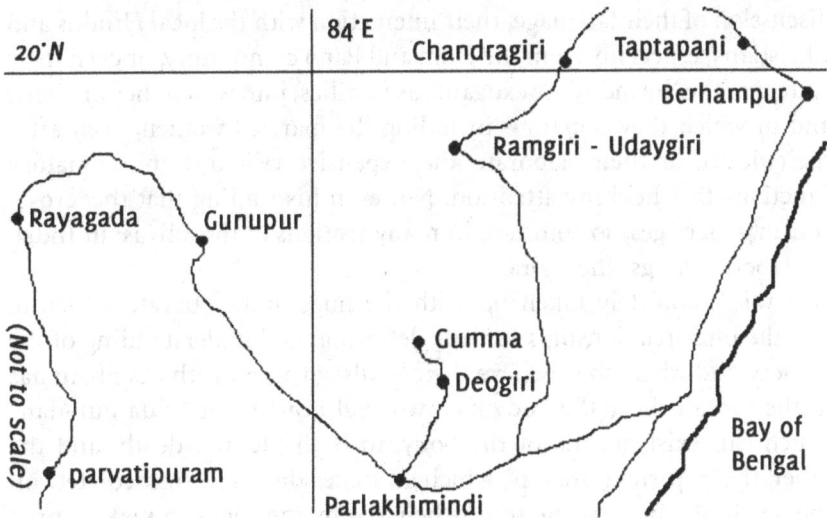

The Ganjam 'Saora' areas

before finally petering out as far away as the Tirupati hills in Andhra and Salem in Tamil Nadu. In these hills have lived since time immemorial large numbers of the 'adivasi' - the original inhabitants of this land – the Santhal, Oraon, Munda, Kharia, Ho, Birhor, Juang, Khond, Koya, Gadaba, Didayi, Bondo, and of course the Saora, right in the middle of them, both literally and metaphorically. According to Dr. S.N. Rajguru, a noted scholar in Parlakimindi, the word is derived from 'Sa', meaning 'with', 'Ora' or original and pristine, and 'An', meaning man.

It had been once again Elwin's writings that had impelled me to make a foray into Ganjam. In his book *The Religion of an Indian Tribe*, he had outlined the social and cultural traits of the Saora, discussing in considerable detail their particular practice of shamanism and belief in an Underworld of ancestral spirits and numerous, and often malignant, gods and demi-gods. The Saora lived here in their mountain fastnesses, preferring the hummocked valleys closeted between hillocks and high plateaus, quite possibly driven there by later immigrants who over the past many centuries settled down to cultivation in the lower valleys and plains. As Elwin has described it, they lived in villages, with the huts built of mud, stone and wood, strung along one longish axis or path, and for all practical purposes, having one common veranda, with one outer room and one inner room for each family. It was not so much Elwin's discussion of their language, their interaction with the local Hindus and Christians, especially from the Dom and Pano community, or even their system of the 'birindas', or exogamous families, into which they are born and in which they remain – including the married women, even after their death, or their elaborate and expensive religious and expiatory functions that held my attention. Not even his finding that the 'cross-cousin' marriages, so common in many sections of the adivasi in India, are taboo amongst the Saora.

I was completely taken up with the huge and elaborate structure and the inter-relationships in their definition and understanding of the Underworld where they believe their 'souls' go after death. As Elwin has it, the Saora believe the body has two souls; one is the 'suda-puradan', which can exist outside of the body, in both life and death, and the other, the 'rup-rup puradan', which animates the body. Immediately on the death of a person, the soul is believed by the Saora to make a brief sojourn into the Underworld (called 'Jaitanadesa'), and after cremation, it moves uneasily from place to place, till the special 'Guar' ceremony is conducted to appease the soul, upon which it becomes a more genial 'ancestral spirit'. More interestingly, this 'Underworld' is very 'real' to the Saora, with its hills, streams, fruiting trees, but seems to be cast always in an eternal half-light, where bears and porcupines do the rounds for their ancestors' protection. It is peopled also by the 'tutelary' spirits who, according to the Saora, live in good houses, and dress and eat well, and are accompanied and assisted by the ancestral spirits, who however live very much like they did before death, somehow gathering food, quarreling amongst themselves and with their unfortunate kin left back in the living world. While the tutelaries live on, growing old and more irascible, the ancestral sprits are thought – so to speak - to be re-incarnated in one part and to stay on in the Underworld in the second part, and there progressively to fade away. This is further complicated by different hierarchies of the Saora gods and deities, from the 'sonumanji', or the gods as conventionally understood, such as 'Darammasum' or the sun-god, or 'Labosum', the earth god. Then there are the 'kittung' or the deities with noticeable human attributes; then there are the tutelaries, who regularly interact with their human spouses, and of course there are the 'kulbanji' or the ancestors, into which a part of the human soul is transformed after the all-important 'Guar' ceremony. Coping with all this are the 'buyya' or the priests who conduct the marriages and funerals, assisted in good part by the village head, the 'gamang', and the all-important 'kuranmaran' or the shaman (often plucking at his 'kuranrajan', a stringed instrument, while chanting) with their respective tutelary wives, each having different powers and therefore performing different functions ranging from interpreting illnesses, unanticipated events, protection against sorcery, damage to harvest and suchlike. Then there are those who perform important religious and social rituals such as the 'Guar' or the 'Doripur'. The Saora are also considerably assisted by female shamanins, who take their tutelary husbands from the Underworld, and who, like the male shamans, perform different rituals against black magic, illnesses and accidents, and participate even in some of the major rituals like 'Guar'. The relationship between the Saora shaman or shamanin and his or her other-worldly tutelary spouse copies in good part the normal relationship between a husband and wife in real life, to the extent of sharing food, providing clothes, and having 'virtual' children. In fact, the individual shaman and shamanin are often married in the real sense and somehow manages to cope with both the earthly and the 'unearthly' marital relationships, of course at some cost to their physical and mental well-being.

A 'kuranmaran' with his 'kuranrajan'

Elwin had dwelt at considerable length on these various beliefs, rituals and functions amongst the Saora in his *The Religion of an Indian Tribe*, but what possibly fascinated him the most were 'séances' or the ritualistic trance-like interaction between a shaman or a shamanin and his or her tutelary spouse and with ancestors to deal with accidental death, illness and the like. The shaman (or shamanin) enters into a trance while performing some repetitive motions such as rubbing a hand on a winnowing fan, and starts a discussion, usually quite acrimonious in the beginning, with the ancestor or the tutelary, and their demands for fish-tail or sago palm (Caryota urens) wine, or clothing, or food having first to be satisfied before they would answer any questions about the cause of the illness or the accident. Threats, pleadings, promises and arguments fly between the affected householder and the ancestor through the mouth of the shaman. In this connection, Khwaja Abdur Razzaq kindly drew my attention to a definitive study of this feature of Saora life in Piers Vitebsky's *Dialogues with the Dead* – a title that quite aptly sums up the situation. Vitebsky had been in Saora country for about eighteen months between 1976 and 1979 and had made a special study of the trance practice of the shaman, recording numerous such séances and the actual verbal thrust and parry between the Saora householder, the shaman and the ancestor or the tutelary.

Elwin had also been fascinated by the Saora practice of drawing votive icons or drawings made with a watery paste of rice powder on the walls of a hut by an 'ittalmaran', or a priest who is empowered to draw the icon or 'ittal'. The inspiration usually comes in a dream to the householder to have a particular icon drawn to propitiate a god or an ancestor. The 'ittalmaran' builds on this basic concept and proceeds to sketch out a 'dream' or wondrous house, with the ancestor or the tutelary riding royally on a horse or an elephant, often having an honorific umbrella over his head, with bands of soldiers escorting him, monkeys and peacock dancing on the roof-top, pots of water, bullocks ploughing fields, trees heavy with honey-combs, with a tiger or a snake or a lizard indicating the particular god in residence.

Such folk paintings have long been known in India, from the pre-historic rock-cave paintings at Bhimbhetka, to the more recent Warli sketches, drawings of Rakha Raja and Rakha Rani in Bastar, the 'pata-chitra' paintings and scrolls of Orissa and West Bengal. Each of these styles has their own fascination, but the sweep of the Saora imagination, compressed into the confines of a sketch measuring just about a couple of feet square, exerted a primeval force on my imagination. Thus, October 1977 saw me putting together a few days to make a foray into the country of the Saora, to see for myself the votive icons that Elwin had seen and written of some thirty years earlier.

As with Bastar, I had little basic information that a traveler needs other than the casual references to place names that Elwin gave in his book, although I now had some maps to go by. Still, it was a bit of a journey into the unknown, as I kept thinking to myself on board the Madras Mail from Calcutta, when early in the morning it swept past the small hillocks by the side of Chilka Lake, that gave the first intimations of the great bundle of hills, spurs and ridges, which make up the Eastern Ghats. By the time I got off at the Berhampur railway station – the rail-head for Parlakimindi – and asked around for the bus stand, it was already mid-morning. By this time I had acquired reasonable skills – after about six years of grounding in Bastar – in boarding country buses, and by about ten o'clock, I was up and away in a bus bound for Parlakimindi. However, as I was soon to find out, boarding a bus is one thing and getting it to move is quite another. One does not necessarily follow the other, not with local (meaning intra-district) buses, and certainly not with buses in rural Ganjam. The conductor behaved as if he was inviting people to a feast, cajoling and pleading with them to board his bus, almost dragging them by the hand from way-side tea-stalls, extolling the 'abundant' standing space, the large window areas to stick heads out of, and indeed the wide open space on the roof and the great speed at which the bus would reach them to their destination. Most of it fell on deaf ears, while some made up their mind – taking their good time about it – and the bus lurched off, only to stop at the next road crossing or bazaar. As if that was not enough, the road wound in and out of the border between Orissa and Andhra Pradesh, and for a time the bus had to stop every now and then at the border check-posts to have its tax and entry papers examined. Thus, it was not till evening that we finally drove into Parlakimindi.

A Saora lady at home

Prosenjit Das Gupta

Interestingly, the town was fairly large and well-ordered, with some fine colleges, as apparently the rulers of what was once a feudatory state were quite enlightened and wanted good education and facilities for their subjects. Some of the colleges and the palace had distinct Gothic architectural features reminiscent of the colleges in Oxford. However, facilities for the casual visitor were conspicuous by their absence, and I almost outdid my Jagdalpur experience by spending the night in one of the most dirty and slovenly boarding-houses that has been my privilege to endure. But then, for four rupees one should not really expect very much more. A bonus was that the owner of the lodge appreciated my interest in the Saora and guided me to Dr. S.N. Rajguru, a well-known scholar in Oriya history, and to Shri Satyanarayan Panda, a noted litterateur of the region. I was privileged to meet them and kept up my connections through correspondence with them for some time.

The next morning – after meeting Dr. Rajguru and Shri Panda – I took the bus to Gumma, which nestles close to the hills where the Saora have many of their villages. Shri Panda had given me an introduction to Shri Bhubanananda Bissoyi, the zamindar of Gumma, and it was with considerable expectation and excitement that I looked up at the passing hills dotted here and there with villages and wondered whether in spite of the uncertainties and hardships I would be able to see any of the Saora icons. Shri Bissoyi maintained a fairly large establishment at the village and on being told of my reference from Shri S.N. Panda, welcomed me cordially, although he was pre-occupied with the impending puja of 'Thakurani', which is held at the same time as 'Durga Puja' celebrated in Bengal and in parts of Orissa, and the Dussehra in north India. Once I was comfortably setup in an outhouse, I went out to see the puja. A small pandal had been erected next to the house; this was more for seating of guests and serving food and refreshments, as the real puja was being held indoors where an assortment of old swords and equally ancient muskets were being propitiated with application of 'sindur', burning of incense and chanting of mantras by the officiating priest.

After lunch, I was introduced to a young lad, Kutano, a Saora, who like many of his tribe even from the days preceding the visits by Elwin, had spent a couple of years in Assam as a tea garden worker. Kutano, who knew a smattering of Hindi besides being quite fluent in Oriya and in his mother-tongue, the Saora language, almost instinctively understood my purpose and that afternoon, we went off towards the west of Gumma, crossing a river and passing through some forests – where, apparently a year later, Khwaja Abdur Razzaq was to pursue a man-eating tiger (and subsequently shoot it in the hills lying to the west of Gumma, opposite Gunupur across the Vamsadhara river). It soon became obvious enough that while there were a number of Saora villages in the locality, those which had largely or wholly converted to Christianity had done away with their earlier practices and had stopped painting the 'ittal', and where there had been any, had covered them over with a clay wash. Although a Christian mission had long been functioning (even before Elwin's visits) in Serango lying to the north of Gumma, devoting their time to the health and general well-being of the Saora, apparently this practice of erasing or defacing the votive icons was a relatively recent phenomenon. So it now became a two-fold task – to find Saora villages amongst those of other communities such as the Pano or the Dom or the caste Hindus, and to ascertain if they were 'Kistan' or 'Indu' (or Hindu, as the Saora disarmingly described themselves). Once we found an 'Indu' village, we then got down to the real business of finding out if any householder had any 'ittal' worth looking at. It was at the village Anukumba, about six or seven kilometres to the northwest of Gumma that we had our first piece of luck. The 'ittal' was not elaborate, unlike the rather elaborate ones described by Elwin. It was drawn with a weak rice paste wash over a rough earthen wall, showing two rows of 'paiks' or armed soldiers on top, with a man carrying pots of water on a bamboo staff over his shoulder at the bottom left and an elephant and a horse at the bottom right. Another icon – in honour of the late mother of the householder and of the Gurpano deity – showed a peacock on top of the square house, trees with honey-combs on either side and a flight of birds (said to have been drawn by Podu Gamang). Yet a third was more elaborate (said to have been drawn by one Rasu Gamang) which depicted a buffalo and a man playing a drum to the left of the house, a langur monkey sitting on top of the house, while a tiger and a couple of 'paiks' or foot-soldiers stood on the right, and a caparisoned horse shaded by an umbrella stood next to them. So, the icons were there, much as Elwin had described, full three decades after he had written about them. Of course, a certain degree of change had come about amongst the Saora and their way of living, but there was also an element of continuity. I felt an immense sense of satisfaction in having been able to see on the dark dingy walls of some of the mud huts, in the weak light of a two-celled torch, those remnants of the soaring beliefs and the artistic imagination of a half-forgotten tribe.

The next morning, Kutano and myself were up quite early. We took the bus that ran from Serango and got down next to the high flank of the Deogiri hill. This rose almost parallel to the road, running approximately north to south, partly covered in scrub and partly in forest, poised like the crest of a wave to crash down on the straggly road below. It was a long and tiring scramble up the hillside, around boulders and along gullies, skirting past high rock faces, higher and yet higher, with the thigh muscles straining and lungs heaving at the unaccustomed strain. Then, in a clearing close to the crest of the hill, we found some Saora ingeniously squeezing oil from oil seeds in a home-made press consisting of a wooden pestle weighed down with a large log tied at one end with several boulders. There were a couple of men, with the typical tightly wound dhoti, with one corner hanging loose at the back, and two or three women, with a short sari around their hips but with no covering over their breasts, with a small brass ring through the septum of the nose, and with the typical German silver spiral threaded through the edge of the ears, as described by Elwin. They were startled by our appearance, for few outsiders ever had any business to visit that trackless wilderness. They were shy and anxious to begin with, but Kutano in his gentle manner soon put them at ease. However, the question that ran around in my mind was whether they would have any 'ittal' worth the effort.

A Saora shaman going into trance

Kutano engaged the group in conversation, explaining who we were and the purpose of the visit, so as to overcome any anxiety on their part; for, tribals were usually wary of visits by officious officials who always demanded food and water for themselves and their retinue. We sat for a while in the shade of the trees, while the oil dribbled from under the pestle set in a rock cup, as the men adjusted the weight of the boulders on the log. Yes, they would introduce us to the 'kuranmaran', or the shaman of the village, and he would explain the rest. So our little group trooped up further along the hillside, till we reached a high, wind-swept plateau, and there stood the village with the typical row of Saora houses, nestling amidst large boulders and occasional trees. Each house had a plinth of three to four feet height and was practically telescoped into each other, much as Elwin had described them. At the center of the wide pathway in between the line of huts on either side stood a Saora shrine, with three or four upright rocks and a tall bamboo pole with an improvised 'umbrella' of grass and twigs at the top to provide a semblance of shade to the deity sheltering amidst the rocks. Thanks to Kutano's introductions, we were received well and given water to wash our faces and to drink, while someone went to call the shaman. He turned up shortly afterwards, a relatively young person of about thirty-five or forty, with an open friendly face. He was quite taken up that anybody should want to climb that hill and ask about 'ittals' and the 'kuranrajan'. Yes, he had one and soon brought it out. It was a flat piece of wood, with a sound box made of the shell of a dried sweet gourd attached at one end, and two strings that are usually plucked by fingers or strummed with a small stick, and a carved head at the other end. It did me a lot of good to be able to see and photograph the instrument that Elwin had written of almost thirty years earlier. It may be said that at least till the 1970s, a considerable population of the Saora were living in Ganjam much as they and their ancestiors had lived in the last few centuries. That the area was sparsely populated and hardly disturbed was clear from the villagers' report that a tiger had killed a bullock at the other end of the village about a week earlier.

From the 'kuranrajan' to the 'ittal', it was not very far. Soon we were led to the home of one of the villagers. Crouching through the low doorway and crowded around by anxious members of the household at this latest 'invasion', with the small torch as the only aid, I could just about discern the outline of a peacock on the top of the 'house', and 'paiks' parading alongside, and the soothing depiction of full honeycombs hanging from a couple of trees outside the sketch of the house. Whoever had drawn it had not been careful with it, using a badly-splayed twig for a brush, and weak rice powder solution. Still, it was something and possibly the climb up the hill would not go in vain. A couple of houses later, we struck gold – at the house of Lakhi, who had had an 'ittal' done in the memory of his mother, Langyen Buyya (wife of the late Mijhi, a 'kuranmaran') – a truly magnificent one, with great fruiting date palms shading the house of the ancestor, a sago palm to one side, with promise of refreshing bliss, a pair of bullocks ploughing the fertile earth, a great snake girdling the house, and stars and a crescent moon providing light to the departed soul. It had all that a Saora ancestor could have wanted. The lines had been delicately done, possibly five or seven years ago (for the weather and termites put their own limits on any pretensions of permanence), with bold arching strokes, with a finely made twig brush and bright white solution of rice powder. I stood for a while in silence in front of the painted shrine, taken in by the leaps of the ittalmaran's imagination and faith. It was the largest (about three feet square) and the finest of the number of 'ittals' that I was to see during that trip and the two subsequent ones.

A Saora votive icon

My second trip to Saora country was once again during the Puja vacations in the following year. This time I broke back from Parlakimindi to the north and east, moving amidst the hills of Ramagiri-Udaygiri. This area is relatively more developed with larger and more settled villages, although the countryside looked barer, with the neighbouring hills practically stripped of their vegetal cover. I left the bus at Ramagiri-Udaygiri town, hardly knowing which way to go, mouthing the magic words 'Saora' and 'ittal' to every shopkeeper and passerby in the hope of some assistance. One kind soul directed me to the local Block Development Office and it was there that I met Shri Balaram Ranahathi, a tall spare man with thinning hair, and a heart of gold. He immediately took me under his wing, much as he had taken his beloved Saora brethren of the neighbouring hills into his personal care. From then onwards it was relatively – note 'relatively' – easy, with a quick round of the neighbouring shops for provisions, putting together a couple of people to carry these and our beddings up into the hills, and we were off. Once out of the fringes of the town, we struck out to the south, down stony pathways, weaving in and out of nullahs, gradually gaining height along the shoulder of a high ridge. While I was making heavy weather of the climb, with my rucksack and so-called 'hunter' boots, Shri Ranahathi, clad in his trade-mark handloom dhoti and kurta and a pair of leather chappals seemed almost in his element as he practically hopped and skipped over or past the boulders, thickets and ravines. We had been climbing for about three hours and evening was coming on when we neared a Saora village sheltering in a shallow boat-like valley between two high ridges. The villagers greeted Shri Ranahathi as the old friend that he obviously was and in no time we were ensconced in one of the rooms with our luggage and provisions. The room was dark and suffocating, so I volunteered to sleep out in the cool of the veranda and as the new moon climbed over the shoulder of the ridge to the east, a cool light transformed that dingy village into a magical place.

Both dinner and sleep come early in a Saora village – indeed in any tribal village in the interior, for there is no light except the natural light of the sun and the moon and human existence has to remain in tune with the passage of day and night and of the seasons. With the assistance of Shri Ranahathi, I was able to visit a number of the huts and see several of the 'ittals'; and photograph them, although they lacked the sweep of imagination of the icon at Deogiri.

The next day, we moved around the village and one of its neighbours, generally taking in the ambience of the Saora villages, with their terraced fields nestling amongst the ridges and ravines, the womenfolk at their routine work of threshing grains, sweeping the hut, caring for children and cooking. It was necessary to appreciate the daily drudgery counterpointed by the elaborate set-up of their beliefs and myths, the playing of the 'kuranrajan', and divinations that may ease, to an extent, their hardship or at least give it some context or perspective. And possibly saw to it that their conditions did not get any worse.

I went for the last time in 1979, this time farther to the northeast of the Eastern Ghats, near the village of Taptapani. This area is well known for its hot springs and many people do visit for this purpose. But few of them know, or cared even if they knew, that there were Saora villages close by, high on the ridge that ran for three or four kilometres to the southwest of Taptapani. So the morning after my arrival, saw me up with the sun, asking around. There were vague replies but the arrival of some Saora down one of the hill paths confirmed that there were villages up there. Well, it was by no means easy to find the path up through the dense thicket of trees – unlike the Saora areas to the west, near Ramagiri-Udaygiri, Tapatapani has greater rainfall. This time I had no Kutano or Ranahathi to give me company and ease the way up, and it was a bit of a struggle to climb about three kilometres diagonally across the face of the hill onto the plateau at the top. As I emerged from the thickets onto the plateau and grasslands, there - about two hundred metres away - was the Saora village, so typically with its telescoped hutments with a common veranda in front, the stone platform in the centre of the courtyard for the gods, the bamboo poles with leaves and a small pot of water for the deities. I emerged slowly and took a slow roundabout way through the patchwork of grasslands and cutivated fields so that the people could see me from afar and not be alarmed. It was almost a replay of Deogiri – with a certain initial anxiety, the menfolk drawing together to stare at me, the women now self-consciously drawing the edge of their short sari to cover their breasts, the children hiding behind their mothers. But the magic word was 'ittal' and that broke the ice, and with a mixture of broken Hindi and Oriya, I was able to convey that I was interested to photograph the 'ittals', and all doors opened. They were really curious and interested that a citified person could actually be interested in their gods and their way of expressing devotion through the painting of the icon. So I was literally led by the hand from one hut to the next. Most of the 'ittals' – and there were not more than three or four – were just some rough sketches, but there was one that was fairly good and well-made.

While all this was going on, a group of Saora started playing on a large tambourine-type of drum in the courtyard in front of the pile of stones for the gods. One of them seemed to go into frenzy, tossing this way and that, his head swaying down and around, then shivering and trembling in his limbs. He was held up by a couple of others and the head of the nearby hut came up to him and whispered in his ears and listened attentively to what the shaman mumbled out. This went on for about eight or ten minutes and then the shaman staggered up and was helped to the veranda of a hut to sit down and to wash his face and limbs. This was the 'dialogues with the dead' that Elwin, and later Vitebsky, had written about. That I could have witnessed this in the hilly fastnesses of Ganjam, despite being so far removed from the days of Elwin, was a matter of some satisfaction.

That evening, having gone with some local villagers of Taptapani to another village to see the conclusion of the Thakurani puja, I was cordially invited by the local priest to walk over the fire pit to show devotion to the deity. In fact, he ran over the burning embers to show off how easy it was. I mumbled my apologies and regretted that my head cold had made me feverish and I was therefore not in a proper condition to display my piety! Then I quickly lost myself in the throng and made my way back under a silent, starred sky.

# 11

# One Last Time

It was in 1984 that I made my last major foray into Bastar. Jaidev, who had given me company, and more, for so many years, had got married and now had his own family. Besides making a new 'pucca' house, he had by now acquired a name for himself for art-metal craft, and had bagged the prestigious President's Award as 'Master Craftsman' a few years earlier. Of course, many more honours were to come his way later. Thus, he now had more responsibilities at home, and ran a studio-cum-workshop and was setting up a self-help society for local craftsmen. The 'Gharwa' community was, however, already shifting in parts from their age-old tradition of 'dhokra' bell-metal crafts to new occupations such as brick-making, driving tractors and so on. Jaidev's father, Shriman, and his mother were both no more. Children were going to school and a new water tap had been installed in the 'mohalla'. A proper lavatory had been built. So, things were changing and, to paraphrase Omar Khayyam, neither my wit nor my tears would lure the 'moving finger' to erase even half a line of what it had already written.

Still, Jaidev was as obliging as ever, and taking leave of his wife, Lata-ji, we were soon on our way to Narainpur as Jaidev – who had not done so earlier - wanted to visit his family deity, Kurmakula Tado, near the village of Tondabeda, deep inside Abujhmarh. That things had indeed changed noticeably was evident from the bus, which now left Narainpur in the morning for Orchha, far removed from the arduous cycle journey that I had undertaken more than ten years ago. The bus journey, cramped up as we were in our seats, was a luxury, saving many hours and aching feet. Soon we were in Orchha, which had transformed from the small village it had been about ten years ago to a bustling settlement of at least ten 'pucca' houses and twenty to thirty huts, with a couple of tea-stalls thrown in for good measure. Of course, the Hill Maria had moved on, deeper into Abujhmarh, content with his little patch of slash-and burn cultivation, a bit of salpi juice, the occasional rice beer, a large field rat or a barking deer for the occasional change of fare. Not for him the torch, umbrella and bicycle that were so dear to the Muria farther to the north, near Narainpur. He was happy to tramp up and down the ridges, along footpaths on his hard, sturdy feet; happy to live in tune with the changing seasons, the rising and setting of the sun and the moon, and the slow traverse of the stars across that great sweep of black velvet sky.

We stopped for a while at Orchha to have a cup of tea and some 'bhujia' and checked that our water-bottles were full – for we had another two or three hours of trek ahead of us – and then we set off. We were travelling light, for we would not spend more than a couple of days at Tondabeda and in a short time the white-painted buildings in Orchha and the murmur of voices in the bazaar were left far behind. It was now down a nullah and up again, skirting along the flank of a ridge, and passing through a short gap between two low hillocks, past forests of sal, mixed with Terminalia, Bauhinia (especially the B. vahlii), Diospyros, Grewia and many other tree species. In those three hours, we did not come across a single person.

Rounding a hill, we came to the shallow valley in which nestled Tondabeda, with a circle of hills all around and patches of slash-and-burn cultivation along the hillsides. There were not more than ten huts in the main village and there were another two or three huts that could be seen further up the hill slopes near the patches of cultivation. We made ourselves comfortable in the ghotul-ghar, made of plaited bamboo, behind a palisade of logs that every Hill Maria home was marked by. Evening was coming on, and we went down to the stream nearby to a wash up and surprised – including ourselves – a couple of Maria lads who were swimming in a rocky pool clad only in their skin. Back in the village, the women busied themselves fetching water, tying up a bullock, or hurrying a child home quite unselfconsciously with their breasts uncovered as they were accustomed to, while I - all too self-conscious - could not even take up the camera to take a picture just for the record.

The next morning, after an early round of tea, Jaidev and I set off to locate his ancestral deity. But Jaidev didn't know much of the Gondi dialect of the Hill Maria, and was making heavy weather of it. Finally, the word 'deoguri' – or place of the gods - seemed to register and we were led about another kilometre away to a thick grove of trees, where under the spreading shade of a mango tree, and sheltered from rain and sun by a small, low open-sided thatch roof, the sheaf of peacock feathers tied to a pole and wrapped in a piece of cloth was pointed out and that was Kurmakula Tado. Jaidev had brought along some plain rice and some puffed rice, and these were offered with due solemnity – but with no ceremony – together with a shining rupee coin to the deity. Then it was back to the village, a quick meal of rice and boiled potato and the return trek to Orchha in time to catch the afternoon bus back to Narainpur.

The next morning we dropped in to look up Belgur, a Muria with whom Jaidev was quite well acquainted, at a village that lay fairly close to Narainpur. He, in turn, gave us the information that there would be a 'nahuni' ceremony at a village about five or six kilometres away, at which stone menhirs would be washed and set up in the memory of some important ancestors. After an early lunch that Belgur's wife quickly arranged, the three of us set out, first along the Narainpur-Chhota Dongar road, and then veering north as the road turned to the south, over fields lying fallow, and then through secondary forests, and then along the bank of a small stream till after an hour or so, we came to the foot of a rocky hillock around which the stream skirted, where in a clearing some twenty villagers, almost all male, were in groups of four or five taking out slabs of stone from the bed of the stream. These were broadly rectangular or triangular in shape, about three or four inches thick and about one to one and half feet along the length and breadth. A party of six or seven women aged about fifty or sixty years were dancing – really more of waving their arms about and skipping around - and singing in the typical falsetto tone, apparently singing the 'relo' and some old ghotul songs, accompanied by four or five drummers, one with a 'madar', two with a sort of large tambourine each, one with a small kettle drum, one giving the occasional toot on a 'tori' bugle, while yet another played the 'muhuri', the local sehnai. This singing and dancing band led the way for the rest of the men towards the village. The men carrying the stones paused now and then and broke into the solemn dirge-like songs that we had heard several years ago at Jharavai village, followed by other motley groups. Soon we neared the village and in a large clearing there were about two hundred people, young and old, men and women standing or sitting around, occasionally having a bit of the 'pej' gruel or sipping 'salpi' as the drummers, singers and the old men carrying the stones arrived and made shallow excavations to set the stones in the earth. Several adult women, about forty or forty-five years of age, were ceremoniously keening while vermillon, mandia 'pej', kosra rice, etc. were being offered to the stone menhirs, and small quantities of water was poured over them. As I later came to know from Belgur – he could speak Halbi and also knew a smattering of Hindi – the 'nahuni' ceremony, as the name suggests, was the setting and ceremonial bathing of stones (called 'pakhna'), usually undertaken in a village once every ten or twelve years, apparently as final propitiation, or a sort of 'pinda daan', as the Hindus have it, to the memory of those who had passed away in the intervening years. It was more a community ceremony in the memory of prominent members of the village or the locality, than by the immediate family of a deceased. Though there was a good bit feasting associated with the 'nahuni', no chicken or pig was found to be sacrificed and interestingly, the dead had reportedly been buried in the vicinity, and not cremated.

We were in luck, for within another couple of days, the 'jatra' or the ceremonial play of the local deity – Khanda Dokra – of the Muria would be held at Belgur's village. The thick pole, with the brass orb on top and the tinsel-decorated red triangle flag that stood for the 'Khanda Dokra' had been brought from Deo Dhanora, a large village near Keskal, accompanied by a number of priests, people clearing the way for the deity by giving the occasional toot from their 'tori' bugle, and the usual camp followers. Primed by quantities of 'salpi' and mahua liquor, the villagers and the guests, boys and girls, men and women spent the night singing, dancing and indulging in a fair amount of horse play, while the priests, or the 'gaitas', had seen their charges – the 'anga' and the 'lat' or deities residing in the decorated poles – come alive and indulge in the 'deo-khel' or the running hither and thither and pushing people over in their exuberance. By the time morning broke, practically everybody was exhausted and had retired to wash up, rest or to cook the morning meal. By late morning, the 'muhuri' players and the drummers had begun to play and the priests bearing their respective 'anga' or 'lat' went from door to door in the village, and were given the occasional drink or some money for their 'bidi' or to buy themselves some drinks.

All good things have to come to an end, and it was no different for me. Going through the books of Elwin, I had been spurred by the idea of seeing and confirming for myself what Elwin had written of more than a generation earlier, firstly about the Muria ghotul and secondly about the Saora pictographs. In the process, I had seen and heard much and had learnt a little about the different terms of references – a 'separate reality' as Carlos Castaneda called it – by which the Muria, the Hill Maria and the Saora live out their lives, closeted amidst their favourite hills and ridges and forests of central and south-central India. These experiences had become a part of me and in no small measure helped to bring into better focus the terms of reference that I had over the years unconsciously drawn up for myself. I did not really wish to wait and witness the progressive merger of these people into the drab 'one-ness' that so many forces of change and development were bringing about. So it was with some degree of satisfaction, tinged no doubt with a bit of sadness, that I bade Jaidev goodbye at his door in Bheluapadar Para in Kondagaon, that had been a second home to me.

I had now seen a good bit of what Elwin had written of. It was time to go after the man himself.

# 12

# Elwin: At Home and at Work

In spite of the biographical details given by Elwin himself in *The Tribal World of Verrier Elwin*, and the more formal biography written later by Ramachandra Guha, I was somewhat dissatisfied. It was as if I was missing out on something: some aspects about Elwin's life, personality and work that had not been mentioned at all, or had been brushed over, or somehow did not hold together properly. In fact, in his autobiography, the scholar mentions being discretely reticent about certain events and maintaining a degree of privacy about himself. This was not enough and I wanted something more – a more detailed, cohesive and rounded view of Elwin. And I certainly needed to know him more fully in the role of the anthropologist that he had slipped into, his research methods and his enormous capacity for study, research and writing, and last but not the least, as a person away from the public eye.

So, after years of tramping about amidst the hills and forests of central India, it was back to the books. There were, of course, the many volumes written by Elwin himself, the few notes – other than obituary references – that had been written about him and some articles specifically about his anthropological researches. Going through them with a tooth-comb needed a sharp focused approach, an equally sharp eye, and of course a good deal of patience. Then followed the meetings and discussions I managed to have with a few of the people who had met or had worked with Elwin personally, and who were alive and able to share their reminiscences. More importantly, there were the discussions and interactions I had with Ashoke Elwin, his youngest son, and Mrs. Lila Elwin, the scholar's second wife. There still seemed to me some missing links, and thanks to information highway via the Internet, and some kindly souls in England, further important bits and pieces could be added. And still one marvellous piece remained, the detailed and annotated bibliography of Elwin, and that came all the way – and surprisingly – from Japan, thanks to the kind interest taken by my good friend, Ms. Akane Kitamura. Then in early 2005, I was given access by Ashoke and allowed to browse through a few of the personal notes and diaries that Dr. Elwin had written in his own hand between 1941 and 1956. Immediately, some aspects of his life that I had only vaguely guessed at came into focus, and a few more facts became known. The persistent questions about Elwin that had swirled around for years in my mind were now beginning to find answers.

First, let us consider what is known about the person. Elwin was tall, about six feet two inches to all accounts, quite robustly built with long legs and arms, and physically strong. His voice was said to be soft but deep in tone. People in most part are largely determined by their birth, training and experiences. Thus, to an extent – but understandably – Elwin was largely defined by the streak of evangelicalism of his immediate parents and family, that posited a sort of loose spiritual fellowship, a sort of brotherhood in Christ. His own father had been called to the cloth, and others on his father's side of the family had also joined the clergy. Elwin himself had trained in theology and for the life of a missionary. At the same time, he had developed a deep and abiding love during his school days for a human and down-to-earth philosophy, beyond conventional faith, through the poems of Wordsworth. He went on to take at Oxford a First Class degree in English Literature in 1924 and again a First in Theology in 1926, most possibly under the tutorship of David Nicol Smith and then under Frederick Wastie Green, respectively. At Oxford, he had become imbued with a spirit of scholarship, not only in the biblical texts but also in a wider moral discourse through the readings of the classics like Plato, Dionysius and others. Poetry, as Elwin himself has admitted, attracted and influenced him considerably – particularly Alexander Pope, the moral essayist and idealistic poet of the eighteenth century, and Swinburne, who had been a stormy petrel and delighted in taking on established beliefs and fashions, especially of the Roman Catholic Church. Another important factor in Elwin's make-up was his attraction for Anglo-Catholicism, which also developed the concept of a divine society to carry forward the mission of Christ for the redemption of mankind from sin. Thus, one could say that to a considerable degree the basic philosophy of life for Elwin was founded on a sense of brotherhood and fellowship beyond a practising faith, in striving to seek the presence of God in everything, and a sense of moral duty and need for atonement. To this were added the strongly humanist thoughts of Rabindranath Tagore and Mahatma Gandhi, about which Elwin came to know through his Sri Lankan friend at Oxford, Bernard Aluwihare. All this and a feeling for the beautiful and the good in things around and about him no doubt constituted a good part of what Elwin himself was and drew him to his work amongst the tribals of India. It should come as no surprise that with this background he should have chosen to begin his work in India (apart for a short duration with the Christa Seva Sangha in Pune) with the treatment and uplift of the lepers in the Central Provinces. No doubt, this sense of brotherhood, humanism and a firm intellectual integrity also contributed to his several scrapes with the diocese at Nagpur and finally, to his quitting the clerical mission and his membership of the Church of England in 1936.

Asceticism came almost naturally to him, what with their own straitened circumstances following the death of his father, his own formal training in Oxford – where he often fasted and spent nights in vigil and prayers – and last but not the least, his days at the Sabarmati ashram of Gandhiji. The same goes for self-help; for they (Elwin and Shamrao Hivale) had to start everything from scratch at the ashram dedicated to St. Francis of Assissi at Karanjia. Elwin has himself added in the TWVE that he used to go on tours barefoot, and never used hair oil (though this changed by the 1940s when he started wearing shoes, or 'Kabuli' chappals on tour), or wore a hat – possibly as a mark of identification with the poor and downtrodden, amongst whom he was then working.

Lest this should lead one to think of Elwin as a 'sadhu', there emerges an element of contradiction. The first inkling of this came to me from a Bengali book, *Dandakarany-er Andhakarey* by Ashutosh Bhattacharyya, a noted linguist attached to the Anthropological Survey of India. In this, he describes how he accompanied Elwin to a visit to the hills of Koraput in western Orissa inhabited by the Bondo tribals, via Jeypore, in 1947. D.V. Sassoon, from a well-known business and philanthropic family of Calcutta, also accompanied them. The object of the visit was to enable Elwin to check up on some events about child-birth amongst the Bondo tribe that he had failed to do on earlier visits. Whatever else he may have practised or the privations he may have suffered while in the Sabarmati ashram of Gandhiji or at Karanjia, Elwin was quite comfortable with the good things of life and was not one to set them aside purely as a matter of principle. He was certainly not averse to a couple of drinks before lunch or dinner and the spicy chicken dishes that the then Maharaja of Jeypore plied them with. This possibly had to do as much with Elwin's own inclinations as the need to ensure that Sassoon, who was used to something rather more than the customary rice, dal and salt that usually comprise a tribal's diet, had better fare. This was again indirectly corroborated by Shri Susanta Chattopadhyay, former chief photographer and cinematographer of the Anthropological Survey of India (whose films on the Toda, the Maria, the Gaddi, the Onge and other tribes of India have to be seen to be believed) who mentioned to me that he had seen Elwin, while working on a project at Manoharpur near the Saranda Hills of south Bihar (now Jharkhand), taking some colourless drink – possibly gin or vodka – quite regularly. This aspect of Elwin becomes fairly established from the occasional mention in his personal notes that he missed his drinks and again that he should try to keep off drinks. Whether the relative isolation from normal social intercourse, that a person of his background and standing looks for, drove him to find solace in regular, and sometimes heavy, drinking is a moot point. There is a reference in the copy of a telegram to Shamrao – possibly somewhat in jest – 'Drink if depressed'. There are also clear – and more than one – references that Shamrao and Sassoon too over-drank often, and is occasionally mentioned by Elwin as having been 'very tight'.

The notes and diaries of Elwin that I was able to glance through are very interesting documents not only for what they reflect about their author, but equally about the social and political life of those days. They are set in large half foolscap paper, with a hard cover, the right-hand pages being filled with the year, date, day of the week and his notes in long hand, with his characteristic rounded script, while the left hand pages are replete with newspaper clippings on various political and social events of those days, copies of some of his book reviews, letters to the editor, match-box labels, quite a few of his personal and official letters, railway tickets, menu cards, invitation cards, and the like. These in themselves are a good indicator of his interests in things other than his immediate work. Elwin has mentioned in the TWVE that 'poulet' was a regular part of the food at Patangarh, and that he had enjoyed smoked salmon, Coq au vin de Sauvignon and crepes flambé on a trip abroad. The number of menu cards in his notes-cum-scrap book indicates that Elwin thought them interesting and important enough to maintain as a record.

Khwaja Abdur Razzaq (who retired as Superintending Anthropologist in the Anthropological Survey of India) recalled that according to several of the ASI staff who had travelled with Elwin (this was of course after 1946 when Elwin was about 44 years of age) he liked to live well in the field, with usually the tehsildar, having charge of the particular block or sub-division, looking after his creature comforts such as accommodation in an inspection bungalow or a good clean hut close to the village chief's home, food and provisions, including the occasional meat or chicken, eggs, supply of water and even the services of a 'dhobi' to wash and iron his trade-mark 'kurta' and 'pyjama'. Of course, it is by no means any impediment to ethnographical work or anthropological research to like one's drinks or the food as offered, or to arrange for fresh and clean clothes. I have enjoyed mahua liquor and fermented 'salpi' juice whenever offered while travelling or staying in Bastar. Chicken was eaten once in about a week or ten days, or even dried fish sometimes, but I drew the line at roasted field rat. Perhaps, in some ways, this helped me to relate to the tribals there and they to me. N.K. Rustamji, former Chief Secretary and later Adviser to the Government of Assam, has also remarked on this aspect of the scholar in his Elwin Memorial Lecture in 1985. Rustamji mentions, in so many words, that Elwin liked his food and his liquor and was quite attracted to women. But the point that strongly emerges is that in spite of his liking for wine and women – if one can put it that way – his scholarship, his genuine interest and commitment in studying and understanding the tribals remained unalloyed. In this, one can again go back to Bhattacharya, who reports that he was hard put to follow Elwin (who was already more than forty-five years of age) on foot over that hilly terrain and spend the better part of the night recording the sequence of events associated with childbirth amongst the Bondo adivasis. So each had its own time and place: the good food and drinks on one side and, the hard work put into research on the other.

From Ramachandra Guha's biography on Elwin, it would appear that

Elwin was by turns attracted to Ala Pocha and Mary Gillet. It is said that he later became interested in Durga Bhagwat, who was also working around that time amongst the tribals of central India. However, as is well-known, Elwin went on to marry Kosi, an 'adivasi' woman in her teens sometime in 1940, when he was already thirty-eight years of age. As Kosi remarks in an interview, Elwin suddenly proposed to her one day and they got married. They had a son, Jawahar, and both the child and Kosi accompanied Elwin during his work and tours in Bastar from 1941 to about 1944. Somehow the marriage did not work out – Elwin was frequently on tour, when according to some reports, Kosi became interested in another man, and he became deeply involved in his writing – and therefore he sought a divorce. This happened in November 1949, and then Elwin married Lila, a Pardhan lady, who had been working for a while at the Patangarh ashram and who would have been just about eighteen or nineteen years of age at that time (she was about seventy five or seventy six years old in 2004). Their first child, Wasant, was born in October 1950. Interestingly enough, some references in Elwin's notes, as late as 1952, indicate that Shamrao, Sunderlal and he himself were not above the occasional – even casual – extra-marital relations. One is left with the thought that perhaps in the days of isolation, far from a social milieu that he had grown up in and was used to for possibly the first thirty years of his life, this was an outlet without which he may have found it difficult to persist in his work in those harsh and demanding circumstances.

Of course, Elwin was not at all a humbug about his fascination for women, and he has – possibly with a bit of tongue in cheek – duly recorded in *The Muria and Their Ghotul*, that the chelik had made a classification of twenty categories of forms of breasts of the motiari, from the 'bondo' or the size of small mushrooms that they regarded with a degree of derision, to the 'hapa', likened to large brinjals, to the 'naral', that is firm and hemispherical. Speaking on All India Radio for the Patel Memorial Lecture, 'A Philosophy of Love', in 1961, Elwin made the forthright declaration that to see women's breasts 'bravely and innocently exposed has always delighted me, not because they excited me sensually, but because they bespeak freedom, health and naturalness'. By that time of course, Elwin was 59 years old and wiser with experience, could quote in the Lecture Fr. M.C. D'Arcy, S.J., 'what was begun in carnality transformed into something spiritual'. Elwin went on to add in this same piece that 'Love illuminates knowledge, gives meaning to beauty, chastens the proud and redeems the sad, the guilty and the ashamed'. So from the enforced celibacy (though possibly with strong undertones of carnal desires) at Gandhi's ashram, to possible relations with more than one woman in the 1930s, to his two successive marriages, to his testimony in the Patel Memorial Lecture, Elwin had walked a full circle.

Another aspect of Elwin's personality also emerges, that of a certain outgoing nature and even of a degree of credulity in his approach towards people, while pursuing his research. Just as he himself had relied on others to get the basic background materials to commence his research – on which more later – Elwin was indulgent to a point in taking on his research trips others such as D.V. Sassoon and Sunil Janah, whose interest and commitment to his work were at best tangential, such as through photography. This was in spite of the fact that Elwin himself admits to possessing a Contax camera with a 50 mm Sonar lens, and an 85 mm lens for close-ups. Although Elwin never grudged it, this may have caused some problems of logistics, food, shelter, etc., in providing for his companions, and even a degree of distraction; though it would be equally true that Elwin after the initial ten or fifteen years of isolation and privation would have looked forward to this companionship.

This also shows up in Elwin's own married life. According to an interview of Elwin's first wife, Kosi, by Raman Kirpal, published in the Indian Express on 15th March 1999, she had been attending Elwin's ashram school at Patangarh during 1939/40, when Elwin, known widely as 'Bada Bhai', expressed his desire to marry her. As Kosi puts it, she would have been about thirteen years of age then, and Elwin was much older. A photograph, which Ashoke Elwin showed me, depicts Elwin dressed up in a turban and tribal attire, sitting gleefully and expectantly on a low platform with a sword in hand, in preparation for the marriage ceremony. Why Elwin at the age of thirty-eight should have decided to marry Kosi, an adivasi girl, who was just about thirteen or fourteen, when he could have married a more mature and educated person from his wide circle of friends and acquaintances in Bombay, is a moot point. Of course, it would have been most unlikely that any wife from such a background would have been prepared to share his life of dedication, deprivation and sheer hard work in the back of beyond place like Patangarh. Kosi and he apparently had two sons, Jawahar and Vijay – although an entry in his diary of 14 July 1947 mentions that 'Kumar and Suresh' are going to school (at Pratt Memorial School in Calcutta, where he was then serving as Deputy Director of the Anthropological Department). According to Kirpal's report, the second was adopted. However, Kosi and her first son indirectly contributed to Elwin's research in Bastar, for they provided a platform and a focus of attention, where the Muria could relate as human beings to Elwin and his family and share their thoughts and experiences. It becomes quite clear from Elwin's tour notes of 1941 that having Kosi and his son on his initial forays into the Bondo hills similarly became useful to build up relationships with members of that tribe. Unfortunately, this marriage did not last. They were divorced in 1949 by an order of the Calcutta High Court – some put it as virtually an 'ex parte' verdict, for Kosi was illiterate and far away in Patangarh. Elwin then married Lila, who he had first met at Patangarh in 1948.

That Elwin was indulgent to a fault with his friends and colleagues is shown up repeatedly. Shri Sushanta Chattopadhyay of the Anthropological Survey of India (ASI) mentions him as an amiable and outgoing personality. Khwaja Abdur Razzaq, also of the ASI, who had also met Elwin - though in passing - mentioned his genial and friendly manner. He would shout when upset about anything, but would very quickly forget and forgive. Apparently, at least in the 1960s, he would good-humouredly refer to younger persons as 'My lad'. Shri Someshwar Lahiri, who had worked as Elwin's steno-typist in Shillong, came to the point of tears when recalling, some fifty years later, his days with Dr. Elwin. He repeatedly referred to Dr. Elwin as being very human and compassionate. Lila Elwin said that Dr. Elwin had taught her "everything". Ashoke, the youngest son, mentioned that in spite of his very busy schedule – Dr. Elwin was then Tribal Adviser to the Government of India and working on a couple of committees reviewing the multi-purpose tribal development blocks – he still found time to take the children out occasionally to see a film at the Kelvin theatre in Shillong, armed with blankets and a flask of coffee. Occasionally, he would take the family out to have a Chinese dinner. A picture of a gentle giant, in physical, intellectual and very human terms, emerges.

One may see further of Elwin's sociable nature and his earnest and sincere ways in the wide circle of well-wishers that had grown up around him over the years. First and foremost were the stalwarts of the Indian freedom movement such Mahatma Gandhi himself (who maintained till the end a personal interest in him), Sardar Vallabhbhai Patel, Jamnalal Bajaj, and later Pandit Jawarharlal Nehru. Without their support and guidance, it is doubtful that Elwin would have been able to embark on his wide-ranging work amongst the adivasis. Then, there were those in Bombay such as J.R.D. Tata, Jehangir P. Patel, and Rustamji Choksi, who stood by him, especially with financial assistance from time to time for his research and publications. There were many that Elwin could call his friends and well-wishers and who had helped or supported him in one way or another since the early 1930s. These included important personages such as M.R. Jayakar, Bhulabhai Desai, Sir Ardeshir Dalal, Jamshed Bhaba, Sir Homy Mody, M.C. Chagla (the noted jurist), John Matthai (a former finance minister of India), and B.G. Kher (a noted administrator), and Thakkar Bapa, the founder of the 'Adimjati Seva Samiti'. He was also close to a circle of renowned journalists or literatteurs such as D.F. Karaka, Shamlal, Sudhin Dutta, Bishnu Dey and Frank Moraes. There was also C.D. Deshmukh (a former finance minister of independent India). Amongst the expatriates, mention may be made of John and Pamela Stent, whose hospitality Elwin enjoyed from time to time (and to whom was dedicated Elwin's first and seminal study *The Baiga* in 1939) and Lindsay Emerson, the then editor of The Statesman, a leading newspaper in Calcutta, and his wife, Minnie. In addition, Elwin had important acquaintances and well-wishers amongst the senior bureaucracy of the country, notably Sir Wilfrid Grigson, Sir J.H. Hutton, W.G. Archer, A.N. Mitchell, all of the exalted Indian Civil Service, Sir Frank Wylie, a former governor of Central Provinces and Ronald Pollock, a judge. There were also Christoph von Fürer Haimendorf, the noted anthropologist from the School of Oriental and African Studies in London, Dr. B.S. Guha and Prof. N.K. Bose, who were later to become Directors of the Anthropological Survey of India. Elwin was equally fortunate in having a circle of committed and dedicated co-workers, notably Shamrao Hivale (his colleague and helpmate since 1932), Sunderlal Narmada Prasad (whom Elwin had practically nurtured since childhood in Patangarh) and later Ashutosh Bhattacharya, Sachin Roy, and Bivas Das Shashtri. Lastly, when working in the north-east, he drew together N.K. Rustamji, Khem Lal Rathi, S.N. Krishnatrey, Yusuf Ali, I.M. Simon and others. Indeed, few have the capability to reach out equally to important public personages, the less exalted and the least known amongst one's circle of friends and well-wishers.

He was able to do this by the simple and common expedient of remaining in touch by visiting them whenever his work would permit and by writing letters – many of them aerograms (now in the British Library archives). He had to go to Bombay every once in a while, either to collect funds for his ashram and school, or for his research or the publication of his books, or to meet R.E. Hawkins of the Oxford University Press, his publishers. Incidentally, Hawkins was around about the same time helping to edit and publish books such as *Man-eaters of Kumaon* by Jim Corbett, the noted hunter. Elwin was a prolific letter-writer, regularly and systematically sending letters to his mother and later to his sister, Eldyth, with whom he was particularly close, and of course, to the others mentioned earlier. Another person with whom Elwin had corresponded – and which had not been earlier taken note of – was with Stith Thompson in the USA, who had, in early 1930s, developed a 'motif-index for folk lore', that is, short descriptive phrases on commonly occurring motifs that could be found in folk tales and folk lore world-wide, and which could be used for comparative purposes. For instance, a reference number was given A0-A99 to the tribal concept of a 'creator', or the number C-199 to sexual taboos, and these could be used for purposes of reference in cross-cultural studies.

It does come as a surprise, therefore, to find that on that dark day of Elwin's death on 23 February 1964, there were few, if any, of his earlier friends and well-wishers by his funeral pyre or later with his bereaved family in Shillong. He had died of cardiac arrest while on a trip to Delhi where he was staying with Khemlal Rathi, and Mrs. Lila Elwin fainted on hearing the tragic news. It was his youngest son, Ashoke, who, at the age of less than ten years, had the duty of lighting the funeral pyre on the banks of a stream near the Polo Grounds in Shillong. Elwin's well-wishers in the ICS and amongst the literati had by then mostly retired and returned to England or had otherwise lost contact. D.V. Sassoon had apparently moved to Thailand and then to Australia and did not keep any contact with the family. Unfortunately, Shamrao Hivale had drifted away by then, possibly due to differences with Mrs. Lila Elwin, with whom he reportedly often had quarrels. It was astounding that try as I might, I could not trace any record of a condolence meeting having been held at the Asiatic Society in Calcutta, despite Elwin having served on their Governing Council and having been awarded the prestigious Annandale Medal by the Society. The obituary columns, at least in the newspapers in India, such as The Times of India and The Statesman seemed quite prosaic and even repetitive, as if copied from one another. It was only in the note by Haimendorf, a copy of which I received courtesy of the Library Services of the School of Oriental and African Studies, London, that a reasonably detailed account of Elwin's life and appraisal of his work can be found. However, this does not really add anything fresh about Elwin as a person and as an anthropologist. It was left to Sachin Roy, Das Sashtri and Someshwar Lahiri to stand by the family in that hour of darkness and help them slowly to start life afresh. In fact, Sachin Roy helped to put together Elwin's collections of tribal artefacts and books and see to their proper preservation at the National Museum in New Delhi. As Ashoke Elwin and Someshwar Lahiri mentioned, Das Shastri, aided to an extent by Jehangir Patel, managed to raise the necessary funds to acquire the residence at Lachaumiere in Shillong for Mrs. Lila Elwin and the children.

These facts also reveal another aspect of Elwin's personality and life: his more or less constantly precarious financial status and the little evidence of providing for his future and his family. Of course, it is only to be expected that having been born the son of a clergy-man, and having himself been educated and trained for a clerical calling, Elwin would have had little wants for himself. His life in the ashram in Karanjia and later in Patangarh had largely been simple and frugal. It is possible that his books since the 1940s brought in a stream of royalties; although it must be remembered at the same time that he had to raise funds from his friends and well-wishers and from Merton College for their publication. However, there is clear evidence that this was by no means adequate and he had at times to turn to his friends, especially Sassoon, or to write book reviews and other articles to make ends meet. Elwin has acknowledged in the Preface to The Muria and Their Ghotul (OUP, 1947) the financial support received from Jehangir Patel, J.R.D. Tata, the Sir Dorabji Tata Trust and the Durbar of the state of Bastar – presumably with the active interest taken by A.N. Mitchell, then Administrator of the state - for the publication (which incidentally was Elwin's doctoral dissertation for Oxford). Similarly, his earlier publication, Folksongs of the Maikal

*Hills* (OUP, 1944) was funded by his old college, Merton, with further assistance by the Government of Central Provinces and Berar, J.R.D. Tata and Jehangir Patel. Merton also assisted in publishing his book, *Myths of Middle India* (OUP, 1949). From the official records available, it seems Merton declined further financial support after 1949. It must be remembered that in 1944, Elwin had been appointed Deputy Director of the Anthropological Department (as it was known then) and was entitled to draw appropriate salary and allowances; although he resigned from the post in 1949 (a diary noting in February 1948 clearly records his disgust at the 'phoney and futile atmosphere' in the Department and his dislike of having to stay in Calcutta). There was a hiatus between that year and 1953 when he was appointed Adviser (Tribal Affairs) to the Government of India, no doubt on appropriate and agreed terms. Despite all this, it seems that he had made little provision for his family in spite of having had an earlier intimation in 1961 of his declining health. He was not particularly interested in his own dressing, and at the time of death in 1964, his cupboard held just three suits, and people recall that he often wore a jacket that had been darned up in places. Prof. Takeshi's bibliography indicates that since about 1950, Elwin had written nearly two hundred reviews and articles, mainly for the Illustrated Weekly of India (IWI), and some for The Statesman, The Times of India and the Marg magazine. Many of these were far removed from his research, although quite within his other interests and learning, such as those on 'Charles Dickens – Studies in Humour' (IWI – 27.7, 1952), 'The Fantastic World of Wodehouse' (IWI – 10.8, 1952) to 'The Last Voyage of the Lusitania' by A.A. Hoehling (IWI – 3.11, 1957). Although, by 1960-61, this huge outpouring of reviews and articles had tapered off – and he reverted to topics related to tribal life - it becomes clear from a reading of Elwin's notes and diaries that he was considerably strapped for cash and this was a source of some anxiety to him. For instance, in January 1952, he records having made Rs. 267 by reviewing books the previous month. Then again, in April of the same year he received Rs. 150 for a feature on the 'Acholi' and writes in protest to the Illustrated Weekly at the paltry sum. In August that same year, Elwin records that since March he had received Rs. 109-6-0 from The Statesman and Rs. 216-12-0 from the The Times of India, and so on.

He had obvious passion for his work – and it was passion, -as Someshwar Lahiri related, Elwin would dictate to him at a stretch for two to two and a half hours from about eight-thirty in the morning, whether on 'A Philosophy for NEFA' or the 600 page 'Report of the Dhebar Committee on multi-purpose tribal development blocks' and other government reports, before turning to other official work, meetings and so on. If there was anything else that kept Elwin going, it was his innate sense of humour. This at least comes out repeatedly even in some of his monographs, such as the one on Bondos, where on one occasion having spent several days waiting for a bus that failed to arrive, he boarded one, which as he put it, really had an engine that worked. In another section in the book, he jocularly observes that it was quite interesting to have so many murderers amongst one's acquaintances, although an anxiety persisted in case one of them should decide to practice on him too. He thought it particularly interesting that the Bondo thought that he had come to enforce prohibition amongst them – which, of course, he did not have the slightest inclination to do! In his study of the Saora religion, he mentions his sense of mortification on being asked, in all innocence by the tribals, if his position was higher than that of the local sub-inspector of police. It is, therefore, no surprise that his autobiography is peppered with such instances where, to begin with, he mentions that he was born on 28th August, the day John the Baptist was beheaded and the day King Herod was born. Further, he wrote that the Saora reportedly sacrifice a goat if they are able to send a forest officer on his way, a fowl for a sub-inspector of police (again!) and a large black pig in the case of an anthropologist! He also mentions having partaken of dishes such as roasted rat amongst the Bondo, chutney of red ants with the Muria and pilaf of dog meat when with the Nagas. He adds that when he was taken in an aircraft to Pasighat to visit the Abor tribe in NEFA, they candidly told him that they were looking forward more to a consignment of pigs. Even when he was quite ill while finishing TWVE, he found it possible to mention that he was on the drug Rawolfia serpentina for high blood pressure, which was also used by the tribals to cure dysmenorrhea, bed-wetting and to ease the delivery of a baby!

A close second to his innate sense of humour that kept him going through all his labours, was his deep interest in reading, especially poetry. There are references in his notes of his browsing through *The Evolution of Marriage* while travelling in a bullock-cart in Bastar, or reading Marlow, de Quincey, Wordsworth, Keats, Milton and Dryden in between his work while at Patangarh. In addition, there were the book reviews to be done, and writing the occasional poems or his manuscripts and doing proof-reading. All this contributed to keeping the body and soul together, and more importantly, to stave off any mental depression.

To supplement and complement his erudition, Elwin had inculcated a strong sense of discipline in all his research and writings. This was greatly facilitated by orderly thought – no doubt inculcated from his undergraduate days in Oxford- and a capacity for 'speed reading'. Both Ashoke and Someshwar Lahiri reported that he could browse through a book in half a day (that is, he could read about two or more books in a day) and pick up the major points or issues. It was the same with his proof-checking; he was able to rush through them and put in corrections and additional notes in the margins by hand. A glimpse of his wide-ranging thoughts and his capacity for working on several ideas at the same time may be found in his introduction to the *Bondo Highlander* (1950), where he mentions working on the publications on tribal myths of Orissa (subsequently published in 1954), the religion of the Hill Saora (in 1955), and on the tribal art of Middle India (in 1951). Even when he was working on his autobiography, he was simultaneously thinking of writing on the Gadaba and the Khond, on whom he had gathered material and 'many photographs'. As Mrs. Lila Elwin related – later corroborated by Mr. Lahiri – Elwin would usually start on his daily work by about seven in the morning, reading through official and personal documents, typing out notes or replies on a trusty – but very battered semi-portable Smith Corona typewriter (which I saw on my last visit to Shillong) – or writing in long-hand; he invariably used Pelican ink. As mentioned earlier, he would usually dictate in connection with his official work for about two to two and a half hours at a stretch to Someshwar Lahiri. Breakfast, and then lunch, would be served in his work or office room. Elwin would sit for hours in his large and battered armchair that was in his office cum work-room, reading or making notes. As later photographs show, he was surrounded by books, more than three thousand of them, and by pictures or images of the Buddha, for Elwin admits to being increasingly drawn to his teachings. Possibly, this was started off by Shamrao confiding to Elwin in June 1952 of becoming a Buddhist. In his later notes, Elwin mentions more than once of a sense of 'mahasukh' or, a sense of deep well-being or bliss. He also started keeping a small image of the Buddha in his pocket and this was with him at his hour of death in 1964. As records with the National Museum in New Delhi show, 3569 books from the collection of Dr. Elwin were gifted by Mrs. Lila Elwin on 21 December 1964, in the presence of Mr. Sachin Roy, then Secretary of the Museum. This collection included a large number of general books on literature, history, etc., besides twenty-seven volumes of 'Man in India' (the journal started by Sarat Chandra Roy) for the period 1922 to 1947, twenty-one volumes of the 'Journal of the Bihar & Orissa Research Society', Bankipur, (1915-1941), the Katha Sarit-sagar by E.M. Penzer, A Grammar of Gondi by C.F.C. Trench, and books by E.M. Thurston, Malinowski, Levi Strauss, and works by Fürer Haimendorf, M.N. Srinivas, Margaret Mead, Franz Boas, Sarat Chandra Roy and some others who had written on tribals. As Mr. Lahiri reports, Elwin had by then taken to smoking cigars, and he would invariably have one stuck in his mouth even as he dictated. Even though this caused his speech to slur slightly, Mr. Lahiri mentioned that he did not really have much difficulty in following the dictation. Elwin would dictate only from short jottings he would have earlier made, without looking at any book or references. Moreover, he had an uncanny capacity, even when interrupted by a telephone call or a visitor, to pick up the thread of the dictation without much ado. Elwin would, later, put in the foot-notes himself, alongside the main text. In all this, Elwin invariably ensured that his personal work was kept separate from his official documentation. He would normally deal with the former himself. He used to have a separate day in the week when he would reply to personal correspondence – at least once a month to his sister Eldyth, and regularly to Minnie and Lindsay Emerson, Christof von Fürer Haimendorf, Arthur Koestler, and many others, besides the occasional book reviews. He invariably bought the stationery separately for this purpose. It was only when he started on his autobiography that he began dictate even on this private enterprise to Mr. Lahiri – but only on Sundays and holidays. He offered to pay Lahiri a monthly stipend for this purpose; but Lahiri had declined, saying that he liked doing the work. Elwin had patted him on the shoulder and had said that he would then do something for him once the book was published. But that was not to be; for the TWVE was published posthumously. When I met Mr. Lahiri much later in 2004, it was clear that the memories of those days were far more precious to him than any monetary gains he may have made.

Such then was the person in private and at work, as others who were close to Dr. Elwin in his last days had seen him, or as he emerges from direct and indirect records. It was now time to see and understand him at work in the field and in his capacity as an anthropologist, or a chronicler – have it whichever way one likes – of tribal life in India.

# 13

# Elwin: In the Field

In taking up to show how Elwin worked on his research in the field, either as an ethnographer or as an anthropologist – depending on the degree of sophistication one would like to have in the definition - reliance has to be placed more on inferences than on direct reports, for there are hardly any direct mentions of his study methods either by Elwin, or by his colleagues, except possibly for the one piece by Ashutosh Bhattacharya. A good bit of the answer, to my mind, lies embedded in his writings. To start off, he wrote a total of eleven books, in some discussing, where so required, at a fairly academic level the aspects of one tribe and then another; in others, making significant compilations of folklore and folk songs. There were also his fictional accounts of life in Gond villages, besides the one covering tribal arts, the official reports and policy papers, and the numerous articles in magazines and learned journals, the occasional monographs and of course, the book reviews as mentioned earlier. By any account, this is a good deal of output for about thirty years of work. Incidentally, just the eleven books specifically dealing with tribal life and culture cover more than five thousand pages – and are not pocket-sized either.

The first hint of how Elwin could encompass such a huge amount of effort is to be found in one of his first books, *Songs of the Forest*: Folk Poetry of the Gonds (George Allen & Unwin, 1935). Here, in the Preface, he mentions that the village and folk songs given in the collection had been selected from about fifteen hundred such songs collected by the Gond Seva Mandal. His helper, companion and in a sense research fellow, Sunderlal Panka (it is not clear if this is the same person as Sunderlal Narmada Prasad referred to in his later books), toured widely to make these collections, and Elwin himself added quite a few from his tours into the Baiga country, accompanied by one S.L. Srikant. Thus, it would seem that a good part – if not the major part – of this and the other compilations were picked up by 'research assistants' and 'research fellows' under the overall guidance and focus given by Elwin. In fact, in this same book, Elwin mentions that the translations of the folksongs were done by 'a syndicate', numbering among them a priest of the Baiga tribe, a Pardhan folk-entertainer, and a cowherd besides Sunderlal and others. The same pattern is repeated in his later book, the *Folk Songs of the Maikal Hills* (OUP, 1944) where again mention is made of Sunderlal, and another Sunderlal (Baghel), and one Rambharose Agarwal, who is mentioned as having collected the songs over many years. Reference was also made by him of the help received from Devendra Satyarthi, who later came to occupy his own place amongst Hindi poets. Further, there is also the reference to the 'Tribal Welfare and Research Unit' (apparently formalised in 1949) in both *Leaves from the Jungle* (OUP, first edition, 1949) and in TWVE, suggesting thereby, that this was another source of data based on which Elwin filled out his respective accounts. In the Introduction to *The Myths of Middle India* (OUP, 1949) Elwin (now with a D.Sc. from Oxford, and as a Fellow of the Royal Asiatic Society of Bengal and Honorary Member of the Ecole Francaise d'Extreme Orient) mentions that a big share of collections was made by the faithful Sunderlal, and by one Gulabdas and Chain Singh, with 'Chhota Bhai', Shamrao Hivale, hovering as always in the background. In the Preface to *The Muria and Their Ghotul* (OUP, 1947), which may well be considered his magnum opus, Elwin mentions the same Gulabdas (now with his title, Dhanuram) for the excellent exploratory work done, the assistance from Shamrao Hivale in gaining a firsthand understanding of Maria life, and of course, the support from a succession of ICS officers in Bastar, from W.V. Grigson himself to E.S. Hyde to A.N. Mitchell. He also refers to the assistance from Thakur Manbahal Singh, the faithful Sunderlal, while Kosi (his first wife, who was from the Gond community herself) filled a major communication gap.

It was hardly any different in his other research publications. In *Bondo Highlander* (OUP, 1950), Elwin mentions that Sunderlal's understanding of the Bondo went deep, and records in so many words that his support as an ethnographic assistant was 'quite admirable'. In addition, there was Gulabdas, and another assistant, Ram Pratap Baghel. Shamrao is mentioned as having made investigations on his own and as having corrected and enlarged Elwin's own impressions and ideas on the Bondo. In *The Religion of an Indian Tribe* (OUP, 1955), Sunderlal once more emerges, this time as 'chief assistant', together with Somra, Gandorbo, Bhajan and Haricharan. In addition, Shamrao was there, and assistance was also received in the field from Ashutosh Bhattacharya, Sachin Roy and others. Even when Dr. Elwin was working in NEFA in 1950s, Sunderlal was constantly by his side (Mr. Lahiri mentioned that he was practically like Elwin's adopted son, so close were they), together with Bhajan, Lahiri himself and an interpreter. Thus, it would not perhaps be drawing an altogether unfair impression, that while Dr. Elwin developed the concepts and gave the overall focus to a particular study, a good deal – or even the major part - of the field-work was done by his associates and assistants.

Secondly, for several of his books, Elwin seems to have depended on earlier studies for some basic data, usually conducted by the concerned government officials. But first things first, ethnographical (in the sense of straight-forward recording of physical, social and cultural features of ethnic or tribal groups) and anthropological (in the sense of more detailed, academic studies on a comparative basis, of a specific aspect of an ethnic or tribal community) work had commenced in India for many years since the work of E.M Thurston and E.T. Dalton in the nineteenth century and linguistic studies by H.H. Risley in the early part of the twentieth century. In a sense, they had been preceded by the references to Indian tribes and castes in the Puranas, and in the 'Katha Sarit-Sagar' or the 'Ocean of Stories' (translated by E.M. Penzer). Sarat Chandra Roy had combined his legal practice and his inquiries into the tribes of the Chhotanagpur region near Ranchi (now in the newly-constituted state of Jharkhand) since 1915 or so, besides starting off the well-known ethnological journal, *Man in India*. Universities at Calcutta and at Bombay had commenced courses in anthropology and in sociology since early 1920s. D.N. Majumdar (with his studies of the Ho tribe), N.K. Bose (who worked on the *Juang of Orissa* in the late 1920s), G.S. Ghurye, K.P. Chattopadhyay amongst others, were distinguished alumni of these faculties. B.S. Guha, who was made Director of the Anthropological Department in 1946 (it was to become the Anthropological Survey of

India later) when Elwin was its Deputy Director, himself had a doctorate in anthropology from Harvard, and gave the presidential address of the anthropological section of the Indian Science Congress in 1928. Thus, by no means can ethnographic or anthropological studies in India be considered to have been virgin territory prior to the arrival of Elwin. It is found that in the Foreword to Elwin's *Maria Murder and Suicide*, Grigson (who incidentally was from St. John's in Oxford) writes that the study has proceeded on the idea that Grigson had himself entertained based on his experiences in the Maria murder trials, and relies on his *The Maria Gonds of Bastar* (OUP, 1938). In the preface to *The Religion of an Indian Tribe*, Elwin refers to the earlier observations and reports on the Hill Saora that he had found in the notes of F. Fawcett to the Anthropological Society of Bombay in 1888, and of G.V. Ramamurti Pantulu (Journal of the Andhra Historical Research Society, 1938), the work of Baron E. von Eickstedt in 1927, and the assistance of Miss A.C.M. Munro of the Canadian Mission in Serango in the Saora Hills.

Not only were source materials and some pointers to the basic thrust of the research taken from earlier workers and administrators, some of the work was undertaken at the express invitation and with the support of Elwin's friends and contacts in the Indian Civil Service (ICS), some of whom were in Oxford more or less at the same time as Elwin. For instance, Grigson (who was his senior at Oxford) invited him to Bastar as early as 1935 to have a look around, and it was from this point that Elwin's interest in the Muria and Maria of Bastar grew. Then there was his dear friend, W.G. Archer, also of the civil service, who had been at Emmanuel College (Cambridge), who took him around the Santhal, Oraon and Munda areas of Santhal Parganas, and in the Chhota Nagpur area of erstwhile Bihar (now Jharkhand). Although J.H. Hutton, also of the ICS, had initially interested Elwin in the Naga hills of north-east India, it was Archer again in late 1940s, who showed him around in that area. Then, there was A.N. Mitchell (who had studied at Balliol, Oxford), once more of the ICS, who arranged to have Elwin appointed as the Census Officer in Bastar in 1941, and thus paved the way for his monumental work on the Muria. It was Mitchell again who introduced Elwin to the Juang, Bhuyan and other tribes of Bonai, Keonjhar and Pal Lahara areas of Orissa and later ensured his appointment as Consultant on Tribal Affairs in Orissa in the mid-1940s. This in turn led to Elwin's work on the Saora and Bondo tribes of that state. This regular interaction between Elwin and some of his friends and acquaintances in the civil service possibly stemmed from the latter's desire to know more about the tribal populations in their charge and to do 'something' for them. It seems logical that this same desire to do 'something' also coloured Elwin's philosophy towards the tribes of India.

He was also well-served by some of his other acquaintances, such as B.S. Kesavan of the National Library in Calcutta. As mentioned in a few places in his diaries, five or six books at a time would be dispatched from the National Library to Elwin in Patangarh – he was very much centred there till about 1952 – and Elwin would read them and keep notes and have them sent back. This speaks as much for the services of the National Library and the Indian Postal Services as about Elwin's search for reference materials.

Even when Elwin himself undertook a survey, it was 'hurry, hurry' all the time. In 'Report of a Tour in the Bonai, Keonjhar and Pal Lahara States' (1942), one of his few field diaries available to the public, Elwin writes of visiting eight Bhuiyan villages in Bonai between 2 and 20 November 1942, then going on to 'do' twenty-six Bhuiyan and Juang villages in Keonjhar from 25 November and several Bhuiyan and Juang villages again from 10 December before rounding off the trip on 22 December 1942. It was more or less the same when he visited the Khond tribal areas in Kalahandi and Koraput in Orissa in 1943 escorted by H.V. Blackburn, as reported in Man in India, Vol. XXIV, 1944. Between 23 November and 9 December 1943, they visited more than eight villages. Even in Bastar, (as mentioned in Appendix 1 of The Muria and Their Ghotul), it is found that of the data on 590 villages that Elwin had checked for ghotul practices, he had personally visited or was familiar with the Muria of only 106 villages. Out of the villages that he had actually visited, the list shows that he spent only a day at 42 villages. While he did have some sort of a permanent camp at Binjhli village (quite close to Narainpur), he seems to have stayed the longest – about 18 days in all – at Kanhargaon. As to the Bondo, he first visited in December 1943, then in March 1945 and in January/February 1946, while Sunderlal and Gulabdas had been sent on initial exploratory missions in 1944 and 1943, respectively. The Saora were first visited in 1944 and then off and on for the next seven years. From The Religion of an Indian Tribe, it appears that he visited particular villages on specific dates to witness some ceremony or the other; such as on 20 April 1946 in connection with the dedication of a female shaman, 13 December 1944 for a pig sacrifice at Bungding village, 19 December 1944 a buffalo sacrifice at Karamsingi, 30 December 1945 to 1 January 1946 at Guli to observe a shaman at work, 18 January 1951 at Taborda to see a divination of an ailment by a shaman, and so on. In this, Elwin differed in his approach significantly from the manner in which earlier anthropologists like A.C. Haddon, Malinowski, Margaret Mead, and Indian scholars like Prof. Nirmal Kumar Bose (in his studies of the Juang) or D.N. Majumdar or even his good friend Haimendorf had conducted their research. It should not also be overlooked that while Elwin largely confined himself to studies on tribes within about four hundred kilometres radius from Patangarh – he never showed any interest in working amongst the tribes in the Western Ghats in southern India. Mead had traveled thousands of miles to far-away Samoa and even Haimendorf had come from his native Germany to study the Chenchus and Reddis of Andhra Pradesh and later, the Naga tribes of north-east India. Later anthropologists like Edward Jay and Piers Vitebsky are also found to have spent fifteen to eighteen months practically at one place amongst the tribals or just in one locality.

One would not be far from wrong, therefore, in holding that what India had gained in the broad extension of knowledge about her tribes through the work of Elwin had been offset to an extent by a certain lack of depth in understanding their cultures and social structures. This lack of academic rigour in Elwin's work has been highlighted by Frank Fernandez (then Assistant Professor in the Department of Sociology and Anthropology at the Brown University, USA) in his article "A Critique of Verrier Elwin's Anthropology", in *Anthropology and Archaeology* edited by M.C. Pradhan, R.D. Singh and others (OUP, 1969). Fernandez, in discussing ethnography and anthropology, has mentioned that the former is descriptive while the latter is analytical. Going further, he mentions that an ethnographer attempts to outline an overview of a society while a social anthropologist is more concerned in studying a society, or an aspect of such a society, with a view to understanding problems of general concern. Thus, in this light, Fernandez holds Elwin to be an ethnographer rather than an anthropologist. He also mentions some differences in the approach and analysis in studies on the Bondo by Haimendorf and that by Elwin. M.C.

Pradhan (Reader in Social Anthropology at the Karnataka Univeristy in Dharwar and later Associate Professor, Department of Sociology and Anthropology, University of Calgary, Alberta) in his article "Verrier Elwin as Anthropologist", in the same book, takes a more sympathetic view. Pradhan deals with Elwin's *The Baiga, The Agaria* and *Maria Murder and Suicide* as studies in the human situation, arising out of exploitation, and the process of change in relation to their respective cultural traits. Elwin's collections of oral literature are placed in a second category, as serving to illustrate the concepts and concerns of those societies. *The Muria and Their Ghotul, Bondo Highlander* and *The Religion of an Indian Tribe* fall in a third category of an honest attempt towards cultural anthropology. In the end, Pradhan points out, Elwin failed to address the institutional set-up and kinship systems in the tribal societies he had described, and this to an extent reduces the value of his work for social and cultural anthropologists. Pradhan makes the pertinent point that Elwin's work was more in the line of Sir James Fraser (of *The Golden Bough* fame) than that of more orthodox anthropologists such as Radcliffe-Brown and Malinowski.

To an extent, this was due to Elwin's lack of any formal training in anthropology and to his own mental make-up and training since his undergraduate days at Oxford. A perceptive comment was made by W.V. Grigson, in the Foreword to *Maria Murder and Suicide* (OUP, 1943), concerning Elwin's work on tribal life, that in addition to his social and philanthropic work, Elwin had now added a sympathetic anthropological dimension to his calling. Possibly because of this, Rustamji has described Elwin as a 'philanthropologist': a combination of a philanthropist and an anthropologist. To be sure, Elwin himself had made no bones about his approach to tribals. This is seen in his fictional works on life of the Gonds in and around Karanjia, in *Phulmat of the Hills* (John Murray, 1937) and in *A Cloud that's Dragonish* (John Murray, 1938) where he speaks of sorcery, jealousy, and of the hills, the sky, and the little modicum of happiness that the tribals were in the process of losing due to the new laws and other societal changes taking place all around. This amalgam of an undergraduate trying to come to terms with what interests him but does not understand fully, the romantic and the missionary in Elwin can also be seen in his first major monograph, *The Baiga*. He is aghast at the exploitation by officials, money-lenders, and even some of the so-called reformed sections of Gonds, and the unseeing and unfeeling laws. For the first time, he is led to consider seriously whether creating 'reserves' for the tribals would not be a bad thing after all; this idea was to dog him through the words and writings of many of his contemporaries, notably G.S. Ghurye, D.N. Majumdar and others, including to an extent, the redoubtable Prof. N.K. Bose.

# 14

# Finally, the Baiga

The questions and issues that raked repeatedly through my mind in those days have quietened. The fever has now abated. Only one final act remained, to complete the circle, so to speak, – to see the Baiga, from where it had all begun.

In spite of having charged up and down central India since about 1970, it was not until the autumn of 2003 that I could arrange a tour of that great mass of hills and forests lying to the north-east of the Chhattisgarh plains and bisected by the Narmada river, where Elwin had lived among and studied the Baiga. I felt no urge to visit Patangarh; for I had learnt that the ashram that Elwin had set up had long perished; only a large 'pipal' tree that had shaded a portion of his compound up on the hill still remained. It was, in any case, more of Pardhan and Raj Gond country, while the Baiga – if they were still to be found – were more likely to be in that great expanse of forests that extended practically from the foot of the Amarkantak plateau to hills and ravines of Pandaria and Baihar. Lots of pilgrims from all over India visit Amarakantak to pay homage at the shrine of Narmada-mai, or the source of the Narmada, one of the great rivers of India, but they have little interest in and less knowledge of the Baiga or where they lived. So, I had to start from scratch once again, from Bilaspur railway junction on the South Eastern Railways, finding the bus and taxi stand, making a deal with a taxi driver who knew something of the area and had a vehicle that would stand up to the driving along the hill roads. Soon we were on our way northwards via Kargi Road and Achanakmar to Kabir Chabutra at the foot of the Amarkantak plateau, from where a road branches off to the west for another ten or twelve kilometres to Karanjia and further on to Patangarh. Elwin had visited

Amarkantak - where the sacred Narmada river has its source in a small spring - more than once and, Kapildhara, where the river leaps down the first of its many falls, on its way more than two thousand kilometres to meet the sea at Gujarat, has been mentioned in TWVE. But would I be able to see the Baiga?

Even after a couple of days of asking around in Amarkantak, I only received vague replies. So on the journey back with a sense of disappointment we stopped the vehicle every now and then to check – but the response was, 'Not here'. We had practically reached Lamni, when next to a grove of trees at some distance from the road, stood Ratan Singh and his small family, Mungli, Kaneria and Suswa. They had that stocky build that Elwin had mentioned and Mungli, who was already past about sixty years, had wizened, parchment-like skin, with the self-same tattoo marks on her chin, cheeks, arms and breasts that Elwin had remarked upon more than sixty years ago. The sari was worn around more as an after-thought than with any particular design. The heavy bunch of bead necklaces told their own story. Even more to the point, Ratan Singh mentioned with more than a touch of regret that they had now taken to tilling the soil 'with bullocks'. The Baiga, as hunters and gatherers who had ranged since time immemorial from Pendra Road in the north and west to Dindori and Mandla, and south to Chilpi and Baihar, along the length and breadth of the Achanakmar and Maikal Hills, driven from the forest fastnesses by laws they had had no hand in framing, had now largely turned to the plough. Even in Elwin's time, this process had started, and he had noted their sense of sadness at having to scour the breast of 'Dharti mata', or the earth goddess, with the sharp iron point of a plough. Soon some neighbours from the nearby huts gathered – for a Baiga village is not a compact unit but scattered over a radius of a couple of hundred metres. There were photographs to be taken and a cup of tea to be had. Inside the thatched huts, the frugal belongings of Ratan Singh and his family were stacked on planks of wood. Some things had changed, but not all of it.

No doubt I felt a certain sense of satisfaction in meeting a Baiga family, and had therefore been able to keep my private tryst with Elwin. But, there was also a touch of sadness that they had had to leave their ancestral lands and could no more roam the forests as they had earlier done. But India was changing and they could hardly be kept totally insulated from this change.

At a tea stall in Lamni, we met Prof. Prabhu Dayal Khera, once of the Delhi University, who in spite of his advancing years had chosen to live amongst the Baiga, to help them stand on their own in a wider and rapidly changing world. It seemed to me, happily, that the tradition of study and service that Elwin had embarked on had now some worthy successors. We left with a promise to return – a promise I am still hoping to fulfill.

# Epilogue

I had been toying with the title that I should give to this section, whether it should be 'In the End', or 'A Final Word'. Neither was suitable; for the story of the Muria and Maria in Bastar, or the Saora in Ganjam or the Baiga in Achanakmar, is by no means over and will play itself out over the next many years, so long as they find refuge in the hills and forests of central India. Change will come – change has already come increasingly over the last fifty years, with the bundles of clothes, aluminium utensils, mirrors, bags of salt and bottles of kerosene brought over by the traders from Kawardha or Parlakimindi or Bilaspur. Change has come stuffed in the tubes of eye ointment and bottles of iodine and mercurochrome at the primary health centre at Orchha. Change has come through that strange thing – the 'ballot box' – that the Maria, Muria, the Saora and the Baiga have trooped to once in five years or so ever since 1952, not knowing or half-knowing how that little box can change so many things. This process of change is impartial – it affects all. Change is also indifferent in that it cares little if it results in good or ill. Possibly on balance, this change has been for the good; for – as a part of personal or national values, take your pick - no human being should be allowed to suffer for want of food or medicines or shelter or water when it is available only a hundred or a hundred and fifty miles away, and materials can be reached by truck or bullock cart or as head-loads.

It is often said as a matter of course that the Muria, Maria, the Saora and the Baiga are 'deprived' and 'exploited'. Deprived of what? Food or shelter? They may be said to be deprived of things like health-care, a modicum of education, or irrigation facilities to grow more crops, which have long been denied to them because of extreme difficulties of reaching these facilities to them in their hilly fastnesses. Or again, because they have been denied their traditional rights to cut trees and bamboo in the reserve forests for their personal use, and because many such trees have been cut by the Forest department and plantations of Eucalyptus are grown instead. Exploited they have been; not in the sense that many of the rural poor in the rest of India have been exploited by landlords and money-lenders. The Muria and Maria and their brethren have often been tricked by traders over the price of clothes or of kerosene, or in the weight of the produce bought or sold. They have also been exploited to some extent by the local police or the excise department over some local land dispute or on account of brewing of their favourite 'landa' or rice beer and 'mahua' liquor at home. In spite of such denial and exploitation, the Muria, Maria, the Saora and the Baiga were a happy, contented and proud lot in the 1970s and 1980s; and that is not a thing to be sneered at. If ignorance is bliss, so be it; for eating the fruit of knowledge may also mean swallowing the worm of greed, jealousy and hatred with it. At least, with their deeply ingrained sense of the community and cooperative living, the Muria, Maria, Saora and the Baiga have largely been spared that.

If the Muria and Maria (and to an extent the Saora and the Baiga) are currently in the news, it is for the wrong reason: because of the activities of Maoist cadres amongst them, and the bloody skirmishes that have occurred from time to time in those areas when the forces of the state go out in search of the Maoists who are said to be running a parallel adminitsration in some places. It is perhaps inherent in most, if not all, ideologies to seek adherents by education, or example or by persuasion, and if all that fails, by coercion. Thus, the Muria, Maria, Saora and the Baiga who are as ignorant of Gokhale and Gandhi as of Marx and Mao, have been drawn willy-nilly into this stand-off between the State and the Maoists and are made to suffer the rigours of revolutionary change that will brook no delay as against the more benign hand of democratic change over time. It is difficult for laymen to understand the weighty difference between 'people's democracy' on the one hand and 'national democracy' on the other. It is the same with these tribals from the heart of India, but they are willy-nilly drawn into the vortex of an intense ideological struggle against the State. Obviously, the Maoists cannot be expected to give up on their ideology just on someone's say-so, any more than the State can walk away from its constitutional obligations. So the people suffer; the more they suffer or are made to suffer, as the revolutionary line of thinking goes, the more propitious times become for a revolutionary overthrow of the government and putting in place a 'people's democracy'. How turns of phrases can influence human thinking! In the process, what was an occasional rape of a tribal woman by a trucker or trader has turned into a rape of cultures, the rape of the soul of a people.

And so the Muria and Maria (and the Saora of the Ganjam Hills and the Baiga near Achanakmar) may have to suffer for some years; as their brethren, the Santhals, Munda, Oraon, Ho, the Kui and the Chenchu and others had to suffer from unknowing and unfeeling laws, from appropriation of their lands by non-tribals, from a callous administration, leading to the occasional revolts against this suffering. So, for a time, the Muria, Maria and their brethren amongst the Saora, Bondo, Baiga, Santhals, Munda, Oraon, and others will have to submit themselves to the Maoist indoctrination camps on the one hand and the Central Reserve Police Force outposts on the other: just a bit of 'collateral damage', with may be a brief mention in the press or as statistics in a government file. And we shall have to wait for some more time before the Muria, Maria, Saora or the Baiga and their brethren find it possible to make their due contribution of dreams and desires, of their gods and heroes, their songs and dances, their arts and crafts to the fabric of India.

# Bibliography

1. Ashutosh Bhattacharyya, "Dandakarany-er Andhakarey", (in Bengali).
2. Nirmal Kumar Bose, "Marriage and Kinship among the Juangs", Man in India, Vol. VIII, 1928.
3. Verrier Elwin, "The Truth about India – Can We Get It?", George Allen & Unwin, 1932.
4. Verrier Elwin and Shamrao Hivale, "Songs of the Forest: The Folk Poetry of the Gonds", George Allen & Unwin, 1935.
5. Verrier Elwin, "Phulmat of the Hills", George Allen & Unwin, 1937.
6. Verrier Elwin, "A Cloud that's Dragonish", John Murray, 1938.
7. Verrier Elwin, "The Baiga", John Murray, 1939.
8. Verrier Elwin, "The Agaria", Oxford University Press, 1942.
9. Verrier Elwin, "Report of a Tour in the Bonai, Keonjhar and Pal Lahara States", British Indian Press, 1942.
10. Verrier Elwin, "Maria Murder and Suicide", OUP, 1943.
11. Verrier Elwin, "Folktales of Mahakoshal", OUP, 1944.
12. Verrier Elwin, "Folksongs of the Maikal Hills", OUP, 1944.
13. Verrier Elwin, "Notes on a Khond Tour", Man in India, Vol. XXIV, 1944.
14. Verrier Elwin, "Folksongs of Chhattisgarh", OUP, 1946.
15. Verrier Elwin, "The Muria and their Ghotul", OUP, 1947.
16. Verrier Elwin, "Loss of Nerve", private publication, undated (circ. 1941).
17. Verrier Elwin, "Myths of Middle India", OUP 1949.
18. Verrier Elwin, "Bondo Highlander", OUP, 1950.
19. Verrier Elwin, "Tribal Myths of Orissa", OUP, 1954.
20. Verrier Elwin, "Religion of an Indian Tribe", OUP, 1955.
21. Verrier Elwin, "Animal Ballet of the Juang", Marg, Vol. XIII, 1959-60.
22. Verrier Elwin, "A Philosophy of Love", Patel Memorial Lectures, 1961.

Prosenjit Das Gupta

23. Fujii Takeshi, "Annotated Bibliography of Verrier Elwin", Tokyo University of Foreign Studies, 1987.
24. Christoph von Fürer-Haimendorf, "Verrier Elwin in India", Library of School of Oriental and African Studies, London, 1964.
25. Christoph von Fürer-Haimendorf, "Dr. Verrier Elwin Memorial Lecture – A Philosophy for NEFA in Retrospect", SOAS, 1968.
26. Wilfrid V. Grigson, "The Maria Gonds of Bastar", OUP, 1949.
27. B.S. Guha, "Some Anthropological Problems in India", address as President, Anthropology Section of Indian Science Congress, Man in India, Vol. VIII, 1928.
28. Ramachandra Guha, "Savaging the Civilised", OUP, 1999.
29. Edward Jay, "A Tribal Village in Middle India", Anthropological Survey of India, 1970.
30. M.C. Pradhan, "Verrier Elwin as an Anthropologist", in M.C. Pradhan, R.D. Singh and others, (eds.), Anthropology and Archaeology, OUP, 1969.
31. Frank Fernandez, "A Critique of Verrier Elwin's Anthropology", in M.C. Pradhan, (eds.), Anthropology and Archaeology.
32. Stephen Fuchs, "Applied Anthropology in India", in M.C. Pradhan, (eds.), Anthropology and Archaeology.
33. Shyamal Kumar Roy, "Bibliographies of Eminent Indian Anthropologists", Anthropological Survey of India, 1974.
34. Russell and Hiralal, "Inscriptions of the Central Provinces", 1932.
35. N.K. Rustamji, "Dr. Verrier Elwin Memorial Lecture", 1970.
36. Stith Thompson, "Motif Index of Folk Literature", Helsinki, 1932.
37. R. Temple, (ed.), "Papers relating to the Aboriginal Tribes of the Central Provinces left in MSS by the late Rev. Stephen Hislop", 1866.
38. Piers Vitebsky, "Dialogues with the Dead", Cambridge University Press, 1993.
39. Jack C. Winslow & Verrier Elwin, "The Dawn of Indian Freedom", George Allen & Unwin, 1931.

9 789383 175918